Readers' Theater, Grade 5: Science and Social Studies Topics

Contents

Introduction 2
Features 3
Index of Reading Comprehension
   and Fluency Skills 6
Correlation to Standards 7

Blackline Masters

Individual Fluency Record 8
Word Cards 9
Facts Chart 10
T-Chart 11
Map of the United States 12
Venn Diagram 13
Word Web 14

Unit 1: Science

The Rescue 15
   A five-character play about a family
   that survives the Asian tsunami—after
   one family member's narrow escape!

Science Alive 29
   A five-character play about kids who
   find a science book in their attic—
   a science book with characters that
   come alive!

The W.H.A.T.E.V.E.R. 43
   A four-character play about friends
   who build a wacky machine for a
   school science project.

Unit 2: Social Studies

A Boston Teapot 57
   A five-character play about a
   grandmother's story of the Boston
   Tea Party—a story told in part by
   the people who lived it.

The Railroad Race 71
   A six-character play about the
   role of immigrants in building the
   transcontinental railroad.

The Hills Are Alive 85
   A six-character play about Mount
   Rushmore's presidents, who
   mysteriously leave the monument
   to learn about modern life.

It's a Capital Idea! 99
   A six-character play about a group of
   students who are touring the nation's
   capital.

Racing the Iditarod 113
   A six-character play about three
   mushers in the Iditarod and the
   reporters who are covering the race.

Answer Key 127

Introduction

Readers' Theater: Science and Social Studies is a program that provides engaging fluency instruction for all your readers!

Students at different reading levels

- Practice the same selections
- Pursue the same instructional goals
- Interact and build fluency together!

Students build fluency through readers' theater plays on science or social studies topics.

Each play has four to six character roles at different reading levels (measured by the Flesch-Kincaid readability scale). Use the reading levels as a guide, not a rule. In some instances, the readability levels may be somewhat misleading, as they are determined in part by syllable count. If a multi-syllable word is repeated frequently in a character's role, the role appears to be at a high reading level. Once the student masters the word, that part of the role is no longer as challenging.

The instructional power of the small mixed-ability group is at the heart of this program. Each play and lesson plan has been carefully designed to promote meaningful group interaction. In contrast to independent reading, readers using *Readers' Theater* build skills in a rich environment of peer-to-peer modeling, discussion, and feedback.

The program provides a clear, structured approach to building fluency, vocabulary, and comprehension. The key to developing skills is practice. Each lesson provides that practice through a routine of five instructionally focused rehearsals.

1. The first rehearsal focuses on familiarizing the students with the overall text.

2. The Vocabulary Rehearsal involves students in various activities focusing on vocabulary words. Use the Word Cards blackline on page 9 to help students master the vocabulary.

3. The Fluency Rehearsal provides explicit fluency instruction focused on one of the following skill areas:
   - Phrasing Properly
   - Using Expression
   - Reading with Word Accuracy
   - Using Punctuation

4. The Comprehension Rehearsal provides explicit comprehension instruction focused on one of the following skill areas:
   - Asking Questions
   - Building Background
   - Identifying Main Idea
   - Making Connections
   - Making Inferences
   - Monitoring Comprehension
   - Summarizing
   - Visualizing

5. The Final Rehearsal brings it all together.

Following the Final Rehearsal, students will be able to perform the play with great confidence and success. Use the Individual Fluency Record on page 8 to provide students with positive feedback.

Readers' Theater 5, SV 9781419031700

Features

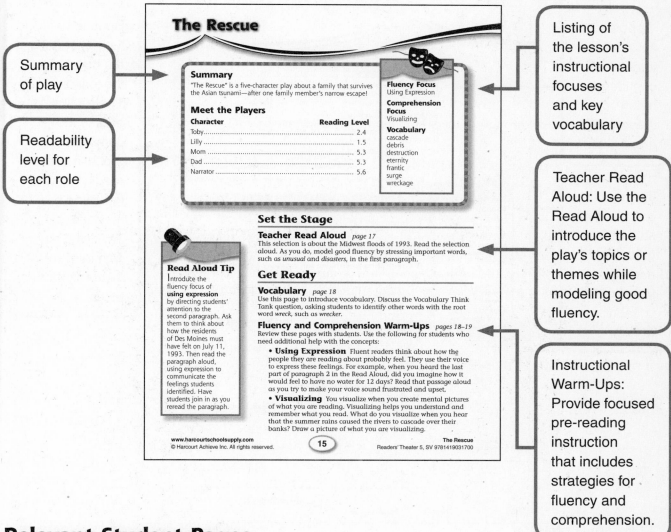

The Rescue

Summary
"The Rescue" is a five-character play about a family that survives the Asian tsunami—after one family member's narrow escape!

Meet the Players

Character	Reading Level
Toby	2.4
Lilly	1.5
Mom	5.3
Dad	5.3
Narrator	5.6

Fluency Focus
Using Expression

Comprehension Focus
Visualizing

Vocabulary
cascade
debris
destruction
eternity
frantic
surge
wreckage

Set the Stage

Teacher Read Aloud *page 17*
This selection is about the Midwest floods of 1993. Read the selection aloud. As you do, model good fluency by stressing important words, such as *unusual* and *disasters*, in the first paragraph.

Get Ready

Vocabulary *page 18*
Use this page to introduce vocabulary. Discuss the Vocabulary Think Tank question, asking students to identify other words with the root word *wreck*, such as *wrecker*.

Fluency and Comprehension Warm-Ups *pages 18–19*
Review these pages with students. Use the following for students who need additional help with the concepts:

- **Using Expression** Fluent readers think about how the people they are reading about probably feel. They use their voice to express these feelings. For example, when you heard the last part of paragraph 2 in the Read Aloud, did you imagine how it would feel to have no water for 12 days? Read that passage aloud as you try to make your voice sound frustrated and upset.

- **Visualizing** You visualize when you create mental pictures of what you are reading. Visualizing helps you understand and remember what you read. What do you visualize when you hear that the summer rains caused the rivers to cascade over their banks? Draw a picture of what you are visualizing.

Read Aloud Tip
Introduce the fluency focus of **using expression** by directing students' attention to the second paragraph. Ask them to think about how the residents of Des Moines must have felt on July 11, 1993. Then read the paragraph aloud, using expression to communicate the feelings students identified. Have students join in as you reread the paragraph.

15

The Rescue
Readers' Theater 5, SV 9781419031700

Summary of play

Readability level for each role

Listing of the lesson's instructional focuses and key vocabulary

Teacher Read Aloud: Use the Read Aloud to introduce the play's topics or themes while modeling good fluency.

Instructional Warm-Ups: Provide focused pre-reading instruction that includes strategies for fluency and comprehension.

Relevant Student Pages

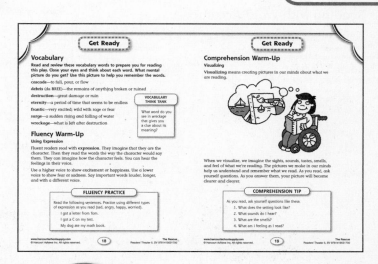

Readers' Theater 5, SV 9781419031700

Features, *continued*

Opportunity for students to build confidence before beginning group work

Tip for engaging student groups in another meaningful vocabulary activity

Routine of five rehearsals, the heart of the lesson. The routine breaks the complex process of oral reading down into simple, manageable activities, each with its own instructional focus.

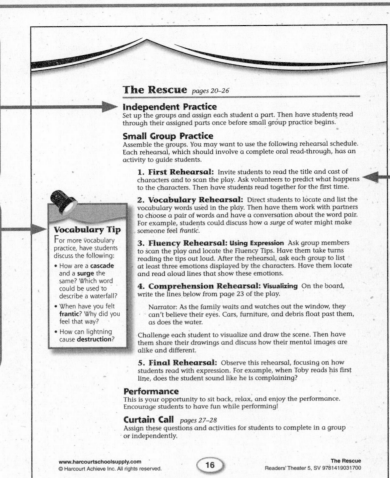

The Rescue *pages 20–26*

Independent Practice

Set up the groups and assign each student a part. Then have students read through their assigned parts once before small group practice begins.

Small Group Practice

Assemble the groups. You may want to use the following rehearsal schedule. Each rehearsal, which should involve a complete oral read-through, has an activity to guide students.

1. First Rehearsal: Invite students to read the title and cast of characters and to scan the play. Ask volunteers to predict what happens to the characters. Then have students read together for the first time.

2. Vocabulary Rehearsal: Direct students to locate and list the vocabulary words used in the play. Then have them work with partners to choose a pair of words and have a conversation about the word pair. For example, students could discuss how a *surge* of water might make someone feel *frantic*.

3. Fluency Rehearsal: Using Expression Ask group members to scan the play and locate the Fluency Tips. Have them take turns reading the tips out loud. After the rehearsal, ask each group to list at least three emotions displayed by the characters. Have them locate and read aloud lines that show these emotions.

4. Comprehension Rehearsal: Visualizing On the board, write the lines below from page 23 of the play.

Narrator: As the family waits and watches out the window, they can't believe their eyes. Cars, furniture, and debris float past them, as does the water.

Challenge each student to visualize and draw the scene. Then have them share their drawings and discuss how their mental images are alike and different.

5. Final Rehearsal: Observe this rehearsal, focusing on how students read with expression. For example, when Toby reads his first line, does the student sound like he is complaining?

Performance

This is your opportunity to sit back, relax, and enjoy the performance. Encourage students to have fun while performing!

Curtain Call *pages 27–28*

Assign these questions and activities for students to complete in a group or independently.

Vocabulary Tip

For more vocabulary practice, have students discuss the following:

- How are a **cascade** and a **surge** the same? Which word could be used to describe a waterfall?
- When have you felt **frantic**? Why did you feel that way?
- How can lightning cause **destruction**?

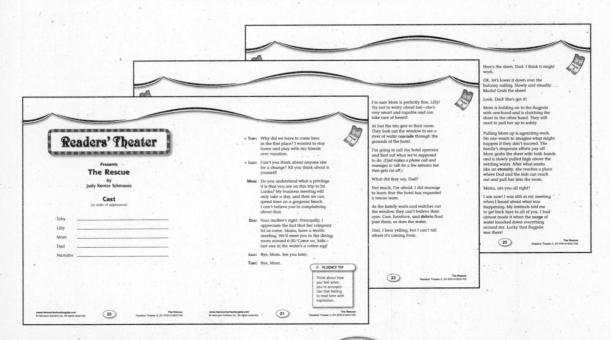

Features, *continued*

Comprehension questions ranging from literal to inferential

Name _____ Date _____

Comprehension

Write your answer to each question on the lines below.

1. Why is the family visiting Sri Lanka? _____
_____

2. What are two signs that warn the family that something terrible is happening? _____
_____

3. What is a tsunami and what is one event that causes it?
_____
_____

4. List the sights, sounds, smells, and feelings the characters probably experienced during the tsunami.
_____
_____

5. What do you visualize when the author writes that "a river of water" cascaded through the grounds of the hotel?
_____
_____

6. How do Dad, Toby, and Lilly rescue Mom?
_____
_____

7. How does Toby's experience help him learn an important lesson?
_____
_____

Vocabulary items testing students' understanding, not their ability to identify verbatim definitions

---

Name _____ Date _____

Vocabulary

Finish the paragraph by writing a vocabulary word on each line.

| destruction surge debris wreckage frantic cascade eternity |

"Paddle harder!" shouted our guide when a (1) _____ of water lifted the raft. We had reached the rapids at last. I felt a little (2) _____ as I tried to steer away from a rock. Our raft bounced from one piece of (3) _____ to the next, narrowly avoiding (4) _____. It seemed like an (5) _____ before we reached calm water.

Extension

Extension activities for additional interaction, involvement, research, writing, and creativity. Use the blackline masters provided on pages 9–14 to help students complete these extension activities.

1. How do you think your family would react in a disaster? Talk with a partner about what you would or would not do.
   • What would you do first?
   • Would you try to save people?
   • Would you stay to try and help survivors, or would you take the next plane home?

2. Choose a partner and do some research on a specific ocean. Find out such things as:
   • How big is that ocean?
   • How deep is it at its deepest point?
   • Where is it located?
   • What kind of marine life calls that ocean home?

Index of Reading Comprehension and Fluency Skills

Reading Comprehension Skills

Skill	Play	Pages
Making Connections	A Boston Teapot	57–70
	The Railroad Race	71–84
Making Inferences	Science Alive	29–42
	The Hills Are Alive	85–98
Monitoring Comprehension	The W.H.A.T.E.V.E.R.	43–56
	It's a Capital Idea!	99–112
Visualizing	The Rescue	15–28
	Racing the Iditarod	113–126

Fluency Skills

Skill	Play	Pages
Phrasing Properly	The W.H.A.T.E.V.E.R.	43–56
	It's a Capital Idea!	99–112
Reading with Word Accuracy	A Boston Teapot	57–70
	The Railroad Race	71–84
Using Expression	The Rescue	15–28
	Racing the Iditarod	113–126
Using Punctuation	Science Alive	29–42
	The Hills Are Alive	85–98

Correlation to Standards

Unit 1: Science

The Rescue *Pages 15–28*

Science Standard: Describes the interactions between human populations, natural hazards, and the environment

Science Alive *Pages 29–42*

Science Standard: Understands the relationships between structures and functions of organisms

The W.H.A.T.E.V.E.R. *Pages 43–56*

Science Standards: Understands the relationship between force and motion
> Understands the physical and chemical properties of matter

Unit 2: Social Studies

A Boston Teapot *Pages 57–70*

Social Studies Standards: Is familiar with important American heroes from the past
> Understands how conflict between the American colonies and Great Britain led to American independence

The Railroad Race *Pages 71–84*

Social Studies Standards: Understands the impact of science and technology on life in the United States
> Understands the contributions of people of various racial, ethnic, and religious groups to the United States

The Hills Are Alive *Pages 85–98*

Social Studies Standards: Is familiar with important American heroes from the past
> Understands the impact of science and technology on life in the United States

It's a Capital Idea! *Pages 99–112*

Social Studies Standard: Understands important customs, symbols, and celebrations that represent American beliefs and principles and contribute to our national identity

Racing the Iditarod *Pages 113–126*

Social Studies Standard: Understands the contributions of people of various racial, ethnic, and religious groups to the United States

Name _____ **Date** _____

Individual Fluency Record

	Needs Improvement	Satisfactory	Excellent
Expression			
Uses correct intonation for statements			
Uses correct intonation for questions			
Uses correct intonation for commands			
Uses correct intonation for exclamations			
Interjects character's emotions and moods			
Reads words in all capitals to express character's emotions			
Reads words in dark print to express character's emotions			
Reads onomatopoeia words to mimic character			
Volume			
Uses appropriate loudness			
Voice reflects tone of character			
Voice reflects feelings of character			
Accuracy			
Reads words accurately			
Speed			
Reads sentences smoothly with line breaks			
Reads words in short sentences as meaningful units			
Reads phrases and clauses as meaningful units			
Reads rhyming text at a constant speed			
Reads rhythmic text with a constant beat			
Punctuation			
Pauses at the end of sentences			
Pauses at commas that follow introductory phrases			
Pauses at commas in series			
Pauses at commas in clauses			
Pauses at commas after introductory names			
Pauses at ellipses			
Pauses at dashes			
Recognizes that question marks are questions			
Recognizes that exclamation points indicate strong feeling			
General			
Demonstrates confidence			
Feels at ease in front of an audience			
Speaks without being prompted			
Speaks at the appropriate time for the character's part			
Demonstrates the character's personality			
Teacher Comments			

Blackline Master: Individual Fluency Record
Readers' Theater 5, SV 9781419031700

WHAT IS THE WORD?
Write the word here.

_____

WHAT DOES THE WORD MEAN?
Write the meaning here.

_____

_____

_____

_____

WHAT DOES THE WORD STAND FOR?
Draw a picture of it here.

HOW CAN YOU USE THE WORD?
Write a sentence using the word here.

_____

_____

_____

_____

_____

Readers' Theater 5, SV 9781419031700

Facts Chart

Topic _____

Facts from the Play	Facts from Other Sources

T-Chart

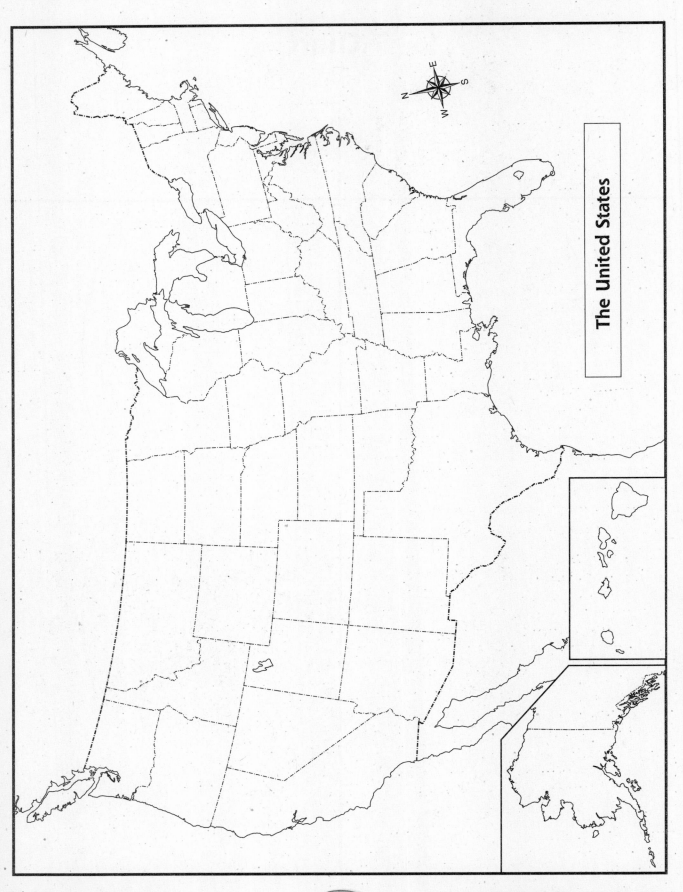

The United States

Blackline Master: Map of the United States
Readers' Theater 5, SV 9781419031700

Venn Diagram

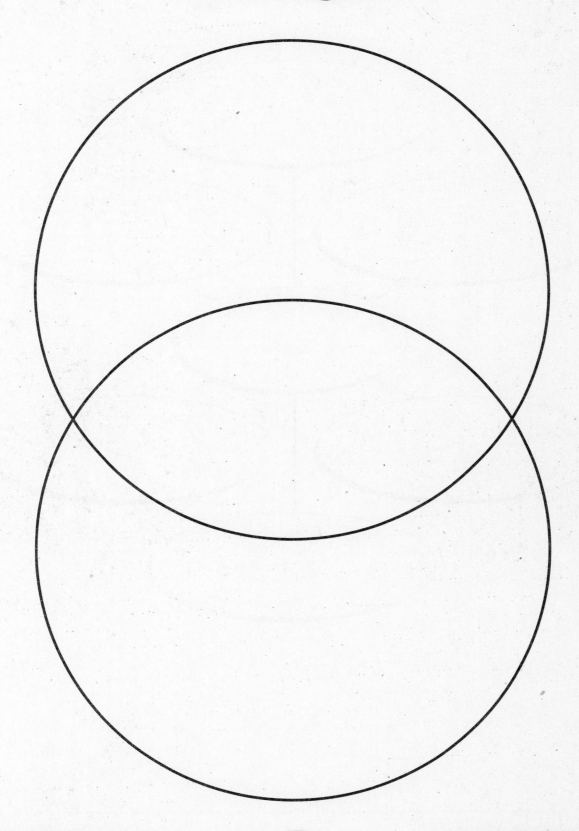

Blackline Master: Venn Diagram

Readers' Theater 5, SV 9781419031700

Word Web

The Rescue

Summary

"The Rescue" is a five-character play about a family that survives the Asian tsunami—after one family member's narrow escape!

Meet the Players

Character	Reading Level
Toby	2.4
Lilly	1.5
Mom	5.3
Dad	5.3
Narrator	5.6

Fluency Focus
Using Expression

Comprehension Focus
Visualizing

Vocabulary
cascade
debris
destruction
eternity
frantic
surge
wreckage

Read Aloud Tip

Introduce the fluency focus of **using expression** by directing students' attention to the second paragraph. Ask them to think about how the residents of Des Moines must have felt on July 11, 1993. Then read the paragraph aloud, using expression to communicate the feelings students identified. Have students join in as you reread the paragraph.

Set the Stage

Teacher Read Aloud *page 17*

This selection is about the Midwest floods of 1993. Read the selection aloud. As you do, model good fluency by stressing important words, such as *unusual* and *disasters*, in the first paragraph.

Get Ready

Vocabulary *page 18*

Use this page to introduce vocabulary. Discuss the Vocabulary Think Tank question, asking students to identify other words with the root word *wreck*, such as *wrecker*.

Fluency and Comprehension Warm-Ups *pages 18–19*

Review these pages with students. Use the following for students who need additional help with the concepts:

- **Using Expression** Fluent readers think about how the people they are reading about probably feel. They use their voice to express these feelings. For example, when you heard the last part of paragraph 2 in the Read Aloud, did you imagine how it would feel to have no water for 12 days? Read that passage aloud as you try to make your voice sound frustrated and upset.

- **Visualizing** You visualize when you create mental pictures of what you are reading. Visualizing helps you understand and remember what you read. What do you visualize when you hear that the summer rains caused the rivers to cascade over their banks? Draw a picture of what you are visualizing.

The Rescue *pages 20–26*

Independent Practice

Set up the groups and assign each student a part. Then have students read through their assigned parts once before small group practice begins.

Small Group Practice

Assemble the groups. You may want to use the following rehearsal schedule. Each rehearsal, which should involve a complete oral read-through, has an activity to guide students.

1. First Rehearsal: Invite students to read the title and cast of characters and to scan the play. Ask volunteers to predict what happens to the characters. Then have students read together for the first time.

2. Vocabulary Rehearsal: Direct students to locate and list the vocabulary words used in the play. Then have them work with partners to choose a pair of words and have a conversation about the word pair. For example, students could discuss how a *surge* of water might make someone feel *frantic*.

3. Fluency Rehearsal: Using Expression Ask group members to scan the play and locate the Fluency Tips. Have them take turns reading the tips out loud. After the rehearsal, ask each group to list at least three emotions displayed by the characters. Have them locate and read aloud lines that show these emotions.

4. Comprehension Rehearsal: Visualizing On the board, write the lines below from page 23 of the play.

> Narrator: As the family waits and watches out the window, they can't believe their eyes. Cars, furniture, and debris float past them, as does the water.

Challenge each student to visualize and draw the scene. Then have them share their drawings and discuss how their mental images are alike and different.

5. Final Rehearsal: Observe this rehearsal, focusing on how students read with expression. For example, when Toby reads his first line, does the student sound like he is complaining?

Performance

This is your opportunity to sit back, relax, and enjoy the performance. Encourage students to have fun while performing!

Curtain Call *pages 27–28*

Assign these questions and activities for students to complete in a group or independently.

Vocabulary Tip

For more vocabulary practice, have students discuss the following:

- How are a **cascade** and a **surge** the same? Which word could be used to describe a waterfall?

- When have you felt **frantic**? Why did you feel that way?

- How can lightning cause **destruction**?

The Rescue

Set the Stage
Teacher Read Aloud

The year 1992 brought an unusual amount of snow to the Midwest. Who would have thought that this white winter blanket would be the cause of one of the worst disasters in the United States?

The snow began to melt in April. Some areas near Des Moines, Iowa, started to flood. By July, the summer rains had caused the Missouri and Mississippi Rivers to cascade over their already high banks. On the morning of July 11, 1993, frantic Des Moines residents awoke to a town almost completely covered by water. Despite the abundance of water outside, there was no clean water inside. The water treatment plant was flooded as well. All 250,000 residents were unable to get clean water for 12 days. No water for showers. No water to drink. No water to flush the toilets.

Nearly 55,000 homes were destroyed by the flood. Fifty people lost their lives. The water finally receded. The water treatment plant was back in service. But the wreckage and destruction were widespread. The entire state of Iowa was declared a disaster area. Debris was everywhere. Thousands of volunteers from the Red Cross came to help. They brought shelter, food, and sanitation facilities. By October, things were mostly back to normal. But no one would forget the flood of 1993.

In this play, you will read about water—its good side and bad. Use the vocabulary and warm-ups to help you get ready.

Vocabulary

Read and review these vocabulary words to prepare you for reading this play. Close your eyes and think about each word. What mental picture do you get? Use this picture to help you remember the words.

cascade—to fall, pour, or flow

debris (da BREE)—the remains of anything broken or ruined

destruction—great damage or ruin

eternity—a period of time that seems to be endless

frantic—very excited; wild with rage or fear

surge—a sudden rising and falling of water

wreckage—what is left after destruction

> **VOCABULARY THINK TANK**
>
> What word do you see in *wreckage* that gives you a clue about its meaning?

Fluency Warm-Up

Using Expression

Fluent readers read with **expression**. They imagine that they are the character. Then they read the words the way the character would say them. They can imagine how the character feels. You can hear the feelings in their voice.

Use a higher voice to show excitement or happiness. Use a lower voice to show fear or sadness. Say important words louder, longer, and with a different voice.

> **FLUENCY PRACTICE**
>
> Read the following sentences. Practice using different types of expression as you read (sad, angry, happy, worried).
>
> I got a letter from Tom.
>
> I got a C on my test.
>
> My dog ate my math book.

Comprehension Warm-Up

Visualizing

Visualizing means creating pictures in our minds about what we are reading.

When we visualize, we imagine the sights, sounds, tastes, smells, and feel of what we're reading. The pictures we make in our minds help us understand and remember what we read. As you read, ask yourself questions. As you answer them, your picture will become clearer and clearer.

COMPREHENSION TIP

As you read, ask yourself questions like these.

1. What does the setting look like?

2. What sounds do I hear?

3. What are the smells?

4. What am I feeling as I read?

Readers' Theater

Presents
The Rescue
by
Judy Kentor Schmauss

Cast
(in order of appearance)

Toby _____

Lilly _____

Mom _____

Dad _____

Narrator _____

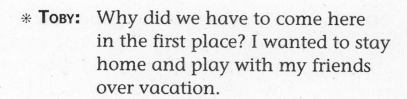

TOBY: Why did we have to come here in the first place? I wanted to stay home and play with my friends over vacation.

LILLY: Can't you think about anyone else for a change? All you think about is yourself!

MOM: Do you understand what a privilege it is that you are on this trip to Sri Lanka? My business meeting will only take a day, and then we can spend time on a gorgeous beach. I can't believe you're complaining about that.

DAD: Your mother's right. Personally, I appreciate the fact that her company let us come. Maria, have a terrific meeting. We'll meet you in the dining room around 6:30. Come on, kids— last one in the water's a rotten egg!

LILLY: Bye, Mom. See you later.

TOBY: Bye, Mom.

> ✳ **FLUENCY TIP**
>
> Think about how you feel when you're annoyed. Use that feeling to read here with expression.

The Rescue
Readers' Theater 5, SV 9781419031700

NARRATOR: And so the unsuspecting family heads down to the beach to soak up the sun and play in the waves. However, later that day . . .

TOBY: Dad, why are those people staring at the water? And what's that awful noise?

LILLY: Daddy, people are starting to run. What's going on?

DAD: I don't know, Lilly. *(Dad stands up and gazes out at the water.)* Oh, no! Let's get out of here! Come on, you guys, grab my hands—we have to get off this beach . . . Right now!

NARRATOR: A terrible tsunami (su NAW mee) was about to hit the beach. A tsunami is a giant wave that's often caused by an earthquake far out at sea.

LILLY: Daddy, I'm scared! Look at the wave! It's going to get us!

TOBY: Come on, Lilly! Grab my hand and hold tight.

NARRATOR: The three run inside their hotel, just as the tsunami breaks on the nearby shore.

LILLY: What about Mom? I want Mom!

Readers' Theater 5, SV 9781419031700

DAD: I'm sure Mom is perfectly fine, Lilly! Try not to worry about her—she's very smart and capable and can take care of herself.

NARRATOR: At last the trio gets to their room. They look out the window to see a river of water **cascade** through the grounds of the hotel.

DAD: I'm going to call the hotel operator and find out what we're supposed to do. (*Dad makes a phone call and manages to talk for a few minutes but then gets cut off.*)

LILLY: What did they say, Dad?

DAD: Not much, I'm afraid. I did manage to learn that the hotel has requested a rescue team.

NARRATOR: As the family waits and watches out the window, they can't believe their eyes. Cars, furniture, and **debris** float past them, as does the water.

TOBY: Dad, I hear yelling, but I can't tell where it's coming from.

LILLY: I hear it, too! It sounds like someone needs help! *(Lilly leans over the railing. She sees a woman holding on to a metal pole. The water is rushing around her. The woman can barely keep her grip on the pole.)*

TOBY: *(sees woman)* That woman is stuck down there, Dad! She's holding on to a metal flagpole. We've got to do something to help her! *(Toby gets a panicked look on his face.)* Dad, it's Mom! The woman holding on to the metal flagpole is Mom!

LILLY: Daddy, please . . . we have to help her! We can't just leave Mom down there like that! She'll drown! *(Lilly bursts into tears.)*

DAD: Go get all of the bedsheets off the beds and knot them together at the corners into one long piece. I'm thinking we can lower the sheet down, and if we're lucky, she'll be able to grab it.

NARRATOR: The **frantic** children run off to do what they're told, while Dad cheers his wife to hold on. He fears she can't hold on too much longer.

> **FLUENCY TIP**
>
> Use loudness and softness to express emotion.

TOBY: Here's the sheet, Dad. I think it might work.

DAD: OK, let's lower it down over the balcony railing. Slowly and steadily . . . Maria! Grab the sheet!

LILLY: Look, Dad! She's got it!

NARRATOR: Mom is holding on to the flagpole with one hand and is clutching the sheet in the other hand. They still need to pull her up to safety.

Pulling Mom up is agonizing work. No one wants to imagine what might happen if they don't succeed. The family's desperate efforts pay off. Mom grabs the sheet with both hands and is slowly pulled high above the swirling water. After what seems like an **eternity**, she reaches a place where Dad and the kids can reach out and pull her into the room.

DAD: Maria, are you all right?

MOM: I am now! I was still at my meeting when I heard about what was happening. My instincts told me to get back here to all of you. I had almost made it when the **surge** of water knocked down everything around me. Lucky that flagpole was there!

LILLY: We're so glad you're safe, Mom. We were so scared!

DAD: Toby and Lilly were amazing, Maria. Obviously, they were terrified, but it didn't stop them. I'm just sorry you had to go through that.

NARRATOR: There's a knock at the door. A team of rescuers takes the family to safety. On the way to the shelter, they hear reports of the **destruction** caused by the tsunami.

MOM: I feel terrible about all those people who've lost everything. The **wreckage** is awful.

TOBY: Mom . . . Dad . . . I have an awesome idea. Do you think we could stay here in Sri Lanka for a while and try to help people? I'd feel really bad going home now.

LILLY: That's an absolutely great idea, Toby! Can we please stay? I want to help, too.

NARRATOR: So the family stayed for as long as they could and did what they could. Everyone, but especially Toby, learned what it was like to think of others.

> **FLUENCY TIP**
>
> Imagine you're the character talking. Match his or her tone of voice and emotions.

Comprehension

Write your answer to each question on the lines below.

1. Why is the family visiting Sri Lanka? _____

_____

2. What are two signs that warn the family that something terrible is

happening? _____

_____

3. What is a tsunami and what is one event that causes it?

_____

_____

4. List the sights, sounds, smells, and feelings the characters probably
experienced during the tsunami.

_____

_____

5. What do you visualize when the author writes that "a river of water"
cascaded through the grounds of the hotel?

_____

_____

6. How do Dad, Toby, and Lilly rescue Mom?

_____

_____

7. How does Toby's experience help him learn an important lesson?

_____

_____

Readers' Theater 5, SV 9781419031700

Vocabulary

Finish the paragraph by writing a vocabulary word on each line.

destruction   surge   debris   wreckage   frantic   cascade   eternity

"Paddle harder!" shouted our guide when a (1) _____

of water lifted the raft. We had reached the rapids at last. I felt a little

(2) _____ as I tried to steer away from a rock. Our

raft bounced from one piece of (3) _____ to the next,

narrowly avoiding (4) _____. It seemed like an

(5) _____ before we reached calm water.

Extension

1. How do you think your family would react in a disaster?
   Talk with a partner about what you would or would not do.

   • What would you do first?

   • Would you try to save people?

   • Would you stay to try and help survivors, or would you take the
     next plane home?

2. Choose a partner and do some research on a specific ocean. Find out
   such things as:

   • How big is that ocean?

   • How deep is it at its deepest point?

   • Where is it located?

   • What kind of marine life calls that ocean home?

Science Alive

Summary

"Science Alive" is a five-character play about kids who find a science book in their attic—a science book with characters that come alive!

Meet the Players

Character	Reading Level
Amy	1.6
David	2.6
Chris	2.3
Dr. Sigmund Science	4.0
Igor Lab	2.1

Fluency Focus
Using Punctuation

Comprehension Focus
Making Inferences

Vocabulary
bacteria
infection
germ
melanin
organ
virus

Set the Stage

Teacher Read Aloud *page 31*
This selection is about the first person to see bacteria through a microscope. Read the selection aloud, modeling good fluency. At the end of each paragraph, stop and reread one sentence, asking students to read along with you.

Get Ready

Vocabulary *page 32*
Use this page to introduce vocabulary. Discuss the Vocabulary Think Tank question. Ask students to support their reasons with facts, if they are able to do so.

Fluency and Comprehension Warm-Ups *pages 32–33*
Review these pages with students. Use the following for students who need additional help with the concepts:

- **Using Punctuation** As you read, look ahead to see what punctuation marks are in your passage. If you see a comma or dash, you know you should be ready to pause. Look at paragraph 3 of the Read Aloud. Find two signals that tell you that a pause is in order.

- **Making Inferences** When reading, you must sometimes figure things out on your own, things that the author doesn't tell you. For example, turn to paragraph 2 of the Read Aloud. Why do you think Leeuwenhoek started making his own lenses?

Read Aloud Tip

Introduce the fluency focus of **using punctuation** by directing students to paragraph 2. Ask students to count along as you note the three commas. Explain that commas are signals for readers to pause. Invite students to reread the paragraph with you, exaggerating the pause at each comma.

Science Alive *pages 34–40*

Independent Practice

Set up the groups and assign each student a part. Then have students read through their assigned parts once before small group practice begins.

Small Group Practice

Assemble the groups. You may want to use the following rehearsal schedule. Each rehearsal, which should involve a complete oral read-through, has an activity to guide students.

1. First Rehearsal: Invite students to preview the play to locate italicized stage directions. Have them practice following the directions at the top of page 36. Then ask students to read together for the first time.

2. Vocabulary Rehearsal: Direct students to locate and list the vocabulary words used in the play. Then have them alternate reading aloud the sentences in which the words appear.

3. Fluency Rehearsal: Using Punctuation Have students review page 32. Then, for the rehearsal, designate one student to be the tip reader. At the end of pages 35 and 37, the tip reader will stop the group, read the tip aloud, and ask another student to apply the tip by reading aloud a relevant section of the play.

4. Comprehension Rehearsal: Making Inferences Suggest that students discuss these questions.
- Why is the book so dusty?
- Why is the book locked?
- Why do you think the author wrote this play?

5. Final Rehearsal: Observe this rehearsal, focusing on students' punctuation. For example, when Chris says, "Look at that!" does the student say the line with excitement?

Performance

This is your opportunity to sit back, relax, and enjoy the performance. Encourage students to have fun while performing!

Curtain Call *pages 41–42*

Assign these questions and activities for students to complete in a group or independently.

Vocabulary Tip

For more vocabulary practice, have students discuss the following:

- Have you ever had an **infection**?

- List two of your body's **organs** and explain what each one does.

Readers' Theater 5, SV 9781419031700

Set the Stage
Teacher Read Aloud

An important part of the story of germs began a long time ago with a man named Anton van Leeuwenhoek (LAY wen hook).

At his job, Anton regularly used a magnifying glass to count the threads in the cloth he sold. Eventually, he became interested in magnifying glass lenses. He even began to make his own lenses. With these fine lenses, Anton was able to build a powerful microscope.

Anton van Leeuwenhoek was not the first person to build a microscope. However, he was the first to build one strong enough to see some very small things. For example, Leeuwenhoek was the first person to see those creepy, crawly things that can make us sick—germs.

There are billions of germs out there. In fact, right now there are probably millions of them on your skin, one of your body's most amazing organs.

In this play, you will learn more about skin and germs. Use the vocabulary and warm-ups to help you get ready.

Vocabulary

Read and review these vocabulary words to prepare you for reading this play. Which words are things that protect you?

bacteria—microscopic cells that can cause diseases

infection—the result of disease getting into body tissues

germ—a common term for bacteria and viruses

melanin—a coloring that occurs in the skin, hair, and eyes

organ—living tissue that serves the body

virus—microscopic cells that cause many diseases, such as the common cold

> ### VOCABULARY THINK TANK
>
> Would you rather be sick with a bacteria or virus? Why?

Fluency Warm-Up

Using Punctuation

Fluent readers read with attention to **punctuation**. They know where the punctuation is and what it stands for. You need to change the way you read based on the punctuation.

When you see a period, stop and take a breath. When you see a comma, make sure you pause. And when you see a question mark or exclamation point, be sure to change your voice to reflect these marks.

FLUENCY PRACTICE

Read the sentences aloud. Watch the punctuation.

1. Before eating, you need to clean the dishes.
2. My sister, who is wearing a green coat, is a lawyer.
3. Ouch! That hurt very badly!

Comprehension Warm-Up

Making Inferences

An **inference** is an educated guess that you make about your reading. To make an inference, use clues in the reading and your own experience.

You must look for clues and then connect them to what you know. One way to practice making inferences is to ask yourself questions as you read. Then you can use what you know to figure out the best answers.

COMPREHENSION TIP

Ask questions like these as you read.
1. What kind of person is this character?
2. Why did the author write this?
3. What will happen next?

Readers' Theater

Presents
Science Alive
by
Laura Layton Strom

Cast
(in order of appearance)

Amy   _____

David   _____

Chris   _____

Dr. Sigmund Science   _____

Igor Lab   _____

AMY: Uggh, I hate Grandma's attic.

DAVID: Oh, it isn't so bad. Mom and Dad said that we might find a real prize or two up here. That makes cleaning it a little more interesting.

CHRIS: All I've found so far is this dusty old book. It seems to be locked. Why would anyone lock a book?

DAVID: Hmm, let me see that book. *(Dusts off cover.)* The title is *Living Science*.

AMY: I love science. That's my favorite subject. Let's open the book.

DAVID: OK, let me work on the lock. *(Makes popping sound with mouth.)* There we go. Wow! Look at the glitter dust coming out of the book. It's landing on the open pages.

✱ **CHRIS:** Look at that! *(Pointing to the book.)* Look at the illustration of the two men in the corner! They are growing. They're . . . they're . . . becoming human!

(Children all take a step back at the same time. Dr. Science and Igor take a step forward.)

> ✱ **FLUENCY TIP**
>
> Remember to pause at the ellipses.

DR. SCIENCE: Well, good day, young ones. Phew! I have not been called out of that book in quite a while. *(Dusts himself off.)*

IGOR: *(with one arm supporting his back)* Oh, Doctor. I think I hurt my backside this time. Ohhh. Eeeee. Uhhhhh.

AMY: Um, sorry, but who are you guys?

DR. SCIENCE: Oh, please allow me to introduce us. I'm Dr. Sigmund Science and this is my assistant, Igor Lab.

IGOR: *(nods)* Pleasure.

DR. SCIENCE: And where is Dr. Cook?

CHRIS: Dr. Cook? Oh, you must mean our grandmother. She is in Africa for a few months helping children there. We are her grandchildren. *(Points to each.)* Chris, Amy, and David. Nice to meet you.

DR. SCIENCE: I'm sorry to have missed your grandmother. She is a special lady. Are you all doctors, too?

AMY: We are not doctors . . . yet. We all love science, though. So what do you usually do when you pop out of the *Living Science* book?

DR. SCIENCE: We come to life and deliver information about science, of course.

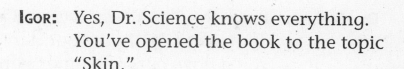

IGOR: Yes, Dr. Science knows everything. You've opened the book to the topic "Skin."

AMY: OK. Please tell us about skin.

DR. SCIENCE: I thought you would never ask.

IGOR: Dr. Science will give you "the skinny" on skin!

CHRIS: "The skinny." Yes, I get it. "The skinny" means he'll give us the facts.

DR. SCIENCE: Right you are. So, do you know which **organ** is the largest in the human body?

DAVID: I might have said the brain. But since the subject is skin, I'm bewildered. Is the skin an organ?

DR. SCIENCE: Yes. The skin is the body's largest organ. It weighs about six pounds. If you could spread your skin out flat, it would be about the size of your bedsheet!

IGOR: Now don't try that at home! Isn't that sickening! Yes . . . sickening.

CHRIS: So what is the point of skin, anyway? Of course, I guess it keeps our guts from falling out!

FLUENCY TIP

Change your voice to express exclamation points.

Readers' Theater 5, SV 9781419031700

DR. SCIENCE: Precisely! Skin does cover and protect our insides. Without your skin, you'd have guts and organs and blood vessels hanging out all over the place. Our skin protects us from **germs**, too. And our skin protects us from heat and cold and from bumps and bangs.

IGOR: Like the bump I took on my backside!

DR. SCIENCE: Exactly! And your skin prevents water loss and protects the body from **infection**. But, some **bacteria** and **viruses** can cause skin diseases.

AMY: The skin also protects us from the sun.

DR. SCIENCE: Very good. The skin makes something called **melanin** that protects you from the sun. The more melanin you have, the darker your skin. When you go in the sun, your skin makes extra melanin to protect you. That is why skin gets darker in the sun. Some people don't make much melanin, so they get sunburns.

DAVID: That would be me! I have to wear a lot of sun protection.

DR. SCIENCE: Smart boy! People who get burned easily can get skin cancer more easily, too.

IGOR: *(shivering)* Thinking about skin cancer gives me the shivers!

CHRIS: That reminds me. How do we get goose bumps on our skin when we shiver?

DR. SCIENCE: Goose bumps happen when the blood vessels get narrow to keep warmth in our body. Then tiny muscles in the skin push up on the hairs on our arms. That makes the hairs stand up straight. That's what we call goose bumps.

IGOR: A hair-raising event, to say the least!

DAVID: So how do we keep our skin healthy, other than wearing skin protection outdoors?

IGOR: Ah, beauty is only skin deep. You must take care of the skin.

DR. SCIENCE: Thank you, Igor. That's an excellent question, David. Your skin is the only organ that needs to be washed regularly. You also can take care of your skin with a balanced diet. Eat your fruits and vegetables. You must also drink enough water. Most doctors recommend six to ten glasses per day! And don't ever, ever smoke.

ALL: Yuck!

Readers' Theater 5, SV 9781419031700

IGOR: *(looks at his watch)* Dr. Science, it is time for us to go. *(Wags finger at kids.)* Now don't be thin-skinned. We have to get back to the lab.

DAVID: Thin-skinned?

AMY: That means sensitive. It is not our fault that they have to leave.

DR. SCIENCE: Yes, we do need to be going. But we'd be happy to come back again and talk about another topic.

CHRIS: Thanks, Dr. Science. That would be great!

IGOR: Put some glitter dust on the book. Then lock it to send us back.

AMY: OK, here you go! *(Makes sprinkling motion with one hand.)*

ALL: Bye!

DAVID: Wow! That was unreal. Let's clean the attic again tomorrow. *(Chris nods yes.)*

AMY: *(nodding yes)* Sounds good to me! Now, don't "skin" your knee on the way down the attic stairs! *(Everyone laughs.)*

Science Alive
Readers' Theater 5, SV 9781419031700

Comprehension

Write your answer to each question on the lines below.

1. Tell two things you learned about skin.

_____

_____

2. What does melanin do?

_____

_____

3. Why do people get goose bumps?

_____

_____

4. List at least two ways to keep your skin healthy.

_____

_____

5. What is your favorite part of this play?

_____

_____

6. How do you think Grandma Cook got the book? Make your own guess.

_____

_____

Science Alive
Readers' Theater 5, SV 9781419031700

Vocabulary

Write each vocabulary word on the line where it belongs.

melanin	virus	bacteria	germs	infection	organ

1. Viruses and bacteria are types of _____.

2. One _____ in your body is the heart.

3. If a wound is not kept clean, you can get a(n) _____.

4. Skin diseases can be caused by a _____ or by

   _____.

5. _____ gives your skin its color.

Extension

1. What would you do if *Living Science* were in your attic? Discuss this with a partner.

   • Would you ask the book a question?

   • What would you ask?

   • Would you share the book with others?

2. With a partner, research another organ of the human body. Compare this organ to the skin. Then present your findings to the class.

The W.H.A.T.E.V.E.R.

Summary

"The W.H.A.T.E.V.E.R." is a four-character play about friends who build a wacky machine for a school science project.

Meet the Players

Character	Reading Level
Narrator	5.7
Nick	2.6
Carrie	4.1
William	5.1

Fluency Focus
Phrasing Properly

Comprehension Focus
Monitoring Comprehension

Vocabulary
assemble
engineer
finesse
kinetic
physicist
potential
versatile

Read Aloud Tip

Introduce the fluency focus of **phrasing properly** by copying the second sentence onto the board. Draw lines to indicate word chunks that would result in improper phrasing, such as, *Energy is never lost—or made, but—. . . .* Read the sentence aloud, using the incorrect phrasing. Then draw new lines to chunk the words properly. Reread and ask students which version they thought sounded better. Then read the sentence together.

Set the Stage

Teacher Read Aloud   *page 45*
This selection is about geothermal energy. Read the selection aloud. Model good fluency, emphasizing proper phrasing by pausing at commas and coming to a full stop at the end of each sentence.

Get Ready

Vocabulary   *page 46*
Use this page to introduce vocabulary. Discuss the Vocabulary Think Tank question. Ask students to name two things an engineer needs to understand about energy.

Fluency and Comprehension Warm-Ups   *pages 46–47*
Review these pages with students. Use the following for students who need additional help with the concepts:

- **Phrasing Properly** One way to phrase properly as you read is to read forward, looking at groups of words rather than each word individually. For example, the fourth sentence in paragraph 2 of the Read Aloud reads, *The eruption of a volcano. . . .* You should read forward to see that the rest of the sentence forms another meaningful phrase. Read this entire sentence aloud.

- **Monitoring Comprehension** Good readers check their comprehension while they read. They ask questions. For example, paragraph 2 of the Read Aloud mentions atoms. If you are not sure what atoms are, you may need to do some research about atoms.

The W.H.A.T.E.V.E.R. *pages 48–54*

Independent Practice
Set up the groups and assign each student a part. Then have students read through their assigned parts once before small group practice begins.

Small Group Practice
Assemble the groups. You may want to use the following rehearsal schedule. Each rehearsal, which should involve a complete oral read-through, has an activity to guide students.

1. First Rehearsal: Encourage students to preview the play by reading the stage directions. Then invite them to read together for the first time.

2. Vocabulary Rehearsal: Have students locate and list vocabulary words used in the play. Then have students choose one word from their lines to teach to the rest of the group. Students can teach the word by giving a definition, acting out the meaning, or giving an example.

3. Fluency Rehearsal: Phrasing Properly Before this rehearsal, ask students to locate and read aloud the Fluency Tips for the play. Have William practice reading aloud his long speech on page 52, with other group members echo-reading each sentence.

4. Comprehension Rehearsal: Monitoring Comprehension During this rehearsal, ask students to monitor their comprehension by concentrating on understanding the different parts of the machine. After reading, challenge them to create an illustration of the machine described on page 51, using words and arrows to identify ramps and levers used in the machine.

5. Final Rehearsal: Observe this rehearsal, focusing on students' phrasing. For example, does William read all expressions inside quotation marks as one phrase?

Performance
This is your opportunity to sit back, relax, and enjoy the performance. Encourage students to have fun while performing!

Curtain Call   *pages 55–56*
Assign these questions and activities for students to complete in a group or independently.

Vocabulary Tip
For more vocabulary practice, have students discuss the following:

- How can being **versatile** make a baseball player more valuable to her team?

- Which are examples of **kinetic** energy: a rolling ball, a bouncing ball, a ball in a box?

- Name two **potential** careers for someone who likes the outdoors.

The W.H.A.T.E.V.E.R.

Set the Stage

Teacher Read Aloud

Everything has some kind of energy. Energy is never lost or made, but it can change, or transform. Here on Earth, everyone uses, sees, or feels energy every day.

Even Earth itself has energy. Thermal energy is heat caused by movement of the atoms and molecules inside something. Geothermal energy, meaning "Earth's heat energy," is an example. The eruption of a volcano is a tremendous display of geothermal energy. The volcano's energy can't be controlled or collected because it is too hot, powerful, and dangerous.

Some geothermal energy is used very safely, however. In a few places, Earth's crust has trapped steam and hot water. Workers drill into the crust and place pipes for carrying the hot water up to a power plant. There, steam from the water turns a turbine generator that changes the energy into electricity.

Homes and schools are using Earth's energy in heat pumps today, too. Plastic pipe is buried underground, going from a building into the ground and back. The pipe is filled with a liquid that conducts geothermal heat well. This liquid flows upward, heating liquid in the building's pipes. An appliance sends the liquid's heat into the building's air. And what happens in summer? The system takes the building's heat underground.

In this play, you will learn more about energy. Use the vocabulary and warm-ups to help you get ready.

Vocabulary

Read and review these words to prepare you for reading this play.

assemble—to put parts together

engineer—an expert in planning and building machines or systems

finesse (fih NESS)—to use careful skill to improve

kinetic (kih NET ik)—of or caused by motion

physicist (FIZ a sist)—a scientist who studies matter and energy

potential—possible

versatile—able to do more than one thing well

> **VOCABULARY THINK TANK**
>
> Why might an engineer need to know some things that a physicist knows?

Fluency Warm-Up

Phrasing Properly

Fluent readers pay attention to the **phrases**, or word groups, in each sentence so that they read faster and more smoothly. A phrase is a group of words that act together to make a whole thought. Chunking, or reading forward through several words at a time, can help you to read more fluently.

If a sentence doesn't make sense, try chunking it differently.

FLUENCY PRACTICE

Read the sentences aloud. As you do, read the words in each word group without pausing.

1. A very large dog / can often bark loudly, / terrifying joggers in the neighborhood.

2. Just in time, / a woman yelled, / "Watch out for the car!"

3. Rico will carefully research / rain forest mammals, insects, and birds / for his project.

Comprehension Warm-Up

Monitoring Comprehension

You need to **monitor** your comprehension or check that you understand each part of a story or article. Good readers monitor their comprehension all the way through their reading.

When good readers don't understand something, they try to get more information. They fix it! They use strategies to help them understand. Understanding makes reading more enjoyable!

COMPREHENSION TIP

Ask yourself questions such as these as you read.

1. Why is this happening?
2. Does this make sense with what I already read?
3. Do I understand this part, or should I reread?

Readers' Theater

Presents
The W.H.A.T.E.V.E.R.
by
Jerrill Parham

Cast
(in order of appearance)

Narrator _____

Nick _____

Carrie _____

William _____

NARRATOR: Two days after Mrs. Lane's assignment, three project partners talk on their way home from school.

NICK: This is getting serious. What machine can we make that no one else has made? We only have a few more days to build it!

CARRIE: Yes, and we can't make just any machine. It must be a compound machine with more than one simple machine in it. It has to use at least two forms of **kinetic** energy.

WILLIAM: We have OUR work cut out for us. Maybe we'll get an idea from our families if we watch them like a hawk.

NARRATOR: Carrie and Nick are used to William using expressions when he talks. He likes playing with words. His friends have nicknamed him "The Wordster." Right now, Carrie and Nick wish they were known as "The **Physicist**" and "The **Engineer**," too . . . But later in three homes, three kids are getting three different ideas.

Readers' Theater 5, SV 9781419031700

NICK: *(to little sister)* Reenie, take only one animal cookie at a time. Hey! That gives me an idea!

CARRIE: *(to dog)* Good going, Pal. That trick earns a treat. Hey! I need a treat dispenser!

WILLIAM: Shazam! I've just cracked a puzzle by watching Mom make an omelet!

NARRATOR: Before school the next day, the partners share their ideas. After school, they get busy trying to draw plans on paper.

NICK: Which machine shall we make? Will it be a treat or cookie dispenser? Or will it be an egg cracker?

WILLIAM: Well, sports fans, let's go for a triple play. Let's look at the big picture. Our one machine can make a treat, a cookie, or anything hard move down a ramp. And at the bottom could be a dog, a child's hand, or an egg. A user can load whatever will be needed. That makes the machine **versatile**. Hey, let's call it The W.H.A.T.E.V.E.R. Machine, short for The Wonderfully Handy, Amazing, Terrific, Enjoyable, and Versatile Energy Ramp Machine!

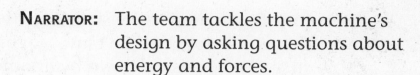

Narrator: The team tackles the machine's design by asking questions about energy and forces.

Nick: *(beginning a sketch)* The whole ramp can be a lever. We can make a flat part at the top of the ramp.

Carrie: Yes, I see. That will be where an object with **potential** energy sits first. The force of gravity will make the object fall when the lever tips down.

Nick: Then the object will have kinetic energy. What could push the lever up on the other end?

Carrie: *(adding to the sketch)* How about a balloon? We could fasten it on a plastic bottle that will inflate it, and then it will push the lever up. I'll make the ramp. Then I'll experiment with chemical energy to fill the balloon with a gas. How can we get a liquid poured to start the chemical action in the bottle?

> **FLUENCY TIP**
>
> Practice phrasing by looking ahead for groups of words to read together smoothly.

WILLIAM: *(pointing to head before sketching)* I've gotten a bolt out of the blue. Maybe a stick can be pushed down by another lever that's like a teeter-totter. The stick could probably tip the liquid's container. I'll work on that section. What can make a string pull up the lever's other end?

NICK: *(sketching)* Maybe the string can be wrapped upward by using wind energy. Maybe we could blow on the machine to start it.

CARRIE: It's a plan. Let's each build our section over the weekend. Then we can put the W.H.A.T.E.V.E.R. together at my house on Tuesday.

WILLIAM: "Knock yourself out," Mr. Physicist and Ms. Engineer! This idea has potential!

NARRATOR: Each friend builds a section alone, adjusting until the section works as planned.

CARRIE: I added a flap where the vinegar flows in. It keeps more carbon dioxide going into the balloon instead of leaking out . . . *(Pouring.)* Yes! The balloon tips the ramp!

FLUENCY TIP

If a sentence doesn't make sense, try chunking it differently.

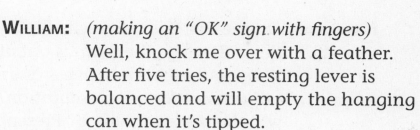

WILLIAM: *(making an "OK" sign with fingers)* Well, knock me over with a feather. After five tries, the resting lever is balanced and will empty the hanging can when it's tipped.

NICK: *(wiping brow)* Phew! I made the paper blades curved and bigger. This helps catch the air. Now I don't have to blow so hard. I can save some of my own energy! It's good that cork is light. It quickly wraps the string.

NARRATOR: Tuesday afternoon is here. It's the day the team will **assemble** the machine. The three partners set all the W.H.A.T.E.V.E.R. sections on a large scrap of wood.

WILLIAM: We seem to need to **finesse** the flow of energy. Isn't "finesse" a great word?

NICK: *(smiling)* I see that my part needs finessing, too.

CARRIE: What will go down the ramp to crack an egg?

WILLIAM: *(pulling something out of a pocket)* This little beauty—a marble from my collection. It's a steelie. It's hard, heavy, and smooth, so it won't be slowed by friction as it rolls.

FLUENCY TIP

In long sentences, read all of a phrase that begins with *on*, *by*, *as*, or *for* before you stop.

NARRATOR: On the first try, the steelie hardly dents the egg. The team is out of time, so they have to guess at an adjustment for the presentation. How will the presentation go? Presentation day arrives. The dog treat and the animal cookie dispensing go well.

WILLIAM: This amazing machine can even crack an egg for you. A steel marble is loaded. Nick, please start the machine.

NARRATOR: The steelie drops a bit hard. Well, let's just say that William's face is very red beneath a lot of runny yellow.

NICK: Oh my! *(To Carrie.)* What is the Wordster muttering?

CARRIE: *(to Nick)* I think I heard him say "guess this shows what 'having egg on your face' means."

WILLIAM: *(wiping off face and speaking to himself)* Oh well. Every cloud has a silver lining. *(Louder, to everyone.)* There's no doubt about it. Energy in the W.H.A.T.E.V.E.R. always does what you wish it to do. Just remember me and be careful what you wish for.

The W.H.A.T.E.V.E.R.
Readers' Theater 5, SV 9781419031700

Comprehension

Write your answer to each question on the lines below.

1. What are two requirements for the machine?

_____

_____

2. How does the machine use chemical energy?

_____

_____

3. How does making the paper blades larger help Nick save energy?

_____

_____

4. Why do you think the machine doesn't work properly when cracking the

egg? _____

_____

5. What is your favorite expression from the play? What does it mean?

_____

_____

6. Why is each friend a good team member?

_____

_____

7. What are the simple machines and kinetic energy used in the play?

_____

_____

Vocabulary

Write the number of a vocabulary word on the line before its meaning.

1. kinetic

2. potential

3. engineer

4. physicist

5. versatile

6. assemble

7. finesse

_____ Able to do many different things

_____ Person who plans and designs machines

_____ Energy of a moving object

_____ Use skill to make something better

_____ To put things together

_____ Possible

_____ Scientist who studies energy

Extension

1. Imagine yourself as a physicist or an engineer. With a partner, talk about your thinking.

   • Which are you, and why?

   • What kinds of projects would you like to do?

   • What would be important about your work?

2. With a partner, research one of the topics below that interests you. Present your findings to the class.

   • What type of energy is used to make electricity in your area?

   • How would you make a safe action toy without a battery or other electrical energy?

   • How are any two forms of kinetic energy alike and different?

A Boston Teapot

Summary

"A Boston Teapot" is a five-character play about a grandmother's story of the Boston Tea Party—a story told in part by the people who lived it.

Meet the Players

Character	Reading Level
Grandma	6.5
Kimiko	4.2
Paul Revere	4.2
Samuel Adams	3.1
Dr. Thomas Young	3.7
Crowd (several students)	4.3

Fluency Focus
Reading with Word Accuracy

Comprehension Focus
Making Connections

Vocabulary
disguised
loyal
Parliament
shipment
unite
volunteer
wharf

Read Aloud Tip

Introduce the fluency focus of **reading with word accuracy.** Explain that fluent readers try to identify and figure out difficult words before reading. To do this, they might look for word parts they know to help them decode the word, or they might look up the word in a dictionary. Invite students to skim paragraph 1 and find two words that they want to figure out before reading.

Set the Stage

Teacher Read Aloud *page 59*
This selection is about the Townshend Acts and American colonists' protests against these taxes. Read the selection aloud. As you do, model word accuracy by pronouncing words correctly.

Get Ready

Vocabulary *page 60*
Use this page to introduce vocabulary. Discuss the Vocabulary Think Tank question, asking students to list three qualities of a loyal person.

Fluency and Comprehension Warm-Ups *pages 60–61*
Review these pages with students. Use the following for students who need additional help with the concepts:

- **Reading with Word Accuracy** If fluent readers encounter unfamiliar words, they look up their pronunciation and meaning. Look at paragraph 3 of the Read Aloud. Point out the word *Massacre*. Check a dictionary to learn the pronunciation and meaning.

- **Making Connections** When you read, you make connections between what you are reading and what you already know. Think about the Read Aloud selection. What is one thing you already knew about colonial protests? How does that idea connect to this selection?

Readers' Theater 5, SV 9781419031700

A Boston Teapot   *pages 62–68*

Independent Practice
Set up the groups and assign each student a part. Then have students read through their assigned parts once before small group practice begins.

Small Group Practice
Assemble the groups. You may want to use the following rehearsal schedule. Each rehearsal, which should involve a complete oral read-through, has an activity to guide students.

1. **First Rehearsal:** Challenge students to preview the play to identify clues that tell when the action switches from modern times to 1773. Have them create the signs described in the stage directions. Then invite students to read together for the first time.

2. **Vocabulary Rehearsal:** Ask students to locate the vocabulary words used in the play and write each one on a separate index card. Then have students take turns choosing and displaying a card, reading the word aloud to the group, and using it in a sentence.

3. **Fluency Rehearsal: Reading with Word Accuracy** Point out the Fluency Tip on page 65. Designate one student as the dictionary reader. Have group members scan their parts for unfamiliar place names. Then have the dictionary reader locate the place names in the dictionary's geographical index and pronounce them aloud for others to echo-read.

4. **Comprehension Rehearsal: Making Connections** Have students work in their groups to create a chart that organizes facts they know about the American Revolution. Encourage students to identify the source of the specific facts whenever possible: from the play, from other sources. Challenge groups to list at least three facts for each column. Use the Facts Chart on page 10.

5. **Final Rehearsal:** Observe this rehearsal, focusing on students' word accuracy. For example, do students reading the colonists' parts correctly pronounce the many proper nouns in their lines?

Performance
This is your opportunity to sit back, relax, and enjoy the performance. Encourage students to have fun while performing!

Curtain Call   *pages 69–70*
Assign these questions and activities for students to complete in a group or independently.

Vocabulary Tip
For more vocabulary practice, have students discuss the following:

- Have you ever been a **volunteer**? What did you volunteer to do?

- Name a time when all the students of this school **unite**. What is their purpose?

- When have you been **disguised**? Why did you wear a disguise?

A Boston Teapot

Set the Stage
Teacher Read Aloud

In the 1700s, it took about two months to sail a ship between England and the American colonies. The colonists started thinking of themselves as separate from England. England did not allow the colonies to elect a representative to Parliament. So when Parliament wanted to tax the colonies, the colonists didn't like it.

In 1767, Parliament passed a set of taxes called the Townshend Acts. The colonists protested. Some of the protests became violent. In Boston, mobs broke windows of stores where English goods were sold. In 1768, England sent soldiers to Boston. The colonists resented the soldiers.

On March 5, 1770, a crowd started shouting at the soldiers. One of the soldiers fired his gun into the crowd. Then eight more soldiers fired. Five colonists died in what came to be known as the Boston Massacre. Two months later the people of Boston learned that on March 5, Parliament had repealed, or gotten rid of, the Townshend Acts.

In this play, you will learn more about another protest against English taxes, the Boston Tea Party. Use the vocabulary and warm-ups to help you get ready.

Readers' Theater 5, SV 9781419031700

Vocabulary

Read and review these vocabulary words to prepare you for reading this play. Say these words to yourself. Then say them each aloud two times.

disguised—wearing a costume to change the way one looks

loyal—faithful; devoted

Parliament—a representative body having the power to make laws in England

shipment—delivery of goods

unite—to bring together for a common purpose

volunteer—one who freely chooses to do something

wharf—a pier or dock where ships tie up and load or unload goods

VOCABULARY THINK TANK

Are you loyal to your friends? How?

Fluency Warm-Up

Reading with Word Accuracy

It is hard to read smoothly and fluently if you do not know the words. Fluent readers read all the words in a story. They learn how to pronounce the words with **accuracy**. They look up unfamiliar words in a dictionary or glossary. If a sentence doesn't make sense, they go back and check that they read all the words correctly.

Remember you need to learn how to pronounce all difficult words, names of people, and names of places. And don't ever skip words.

FLUENCY PRACTICE

Practice reading these sentences aloud. Do not skip words.

1. They did not like "taxation without representation."
2. Samuel Adams was a leader in Boston, Massachusetts.
3. Parliament made laws in England.

Comprehension Warm-Up

Making Connections

When you think about how one story is like another story, you are **making connections**. You can connect ideas from one book with other things you know.

You can connect what you are reading to another book you have read. You can connect what you are reading to something that has happened to you. You also can connect what you are reading to something happening in the world.

COMPREHENSION TIP

Ask yourself questions like these when you read.

1. How does this story remind me of other stories I've read?

2. How do my feelings compare to this character's feelings?

3. How do the events in this story fit with what I know about the world?

Readers' Theater 5, SV 9781419031700

Readers' Theater

Presents

A Boston Teapot

by
Carol M. Elliott

Cast

(in order of appearance)

Grandma _____

Kimiko _____

Paul Revere _____

Samuel Adams _____

Dr. Thomas Young _____

Crowd _____

_____

_____

_____

_____

GRANDMA: Hello, Kimiko. What are you studying?

KIMIKO: Social studies. We're reading about the Boston Tea Party. But Grandma, I don't understand it. Why did Native Americans want to throw tea into Boston Harbor?

GRANDMA: I think you misunderstood what you read. The men who took part in the Boston Tea Party were **disguised** as Native Americans, but they were really colonists.

KIMIKO: Why were they disguised?

GRANDMA: So they wouldn't get into trouble for destroying the tea. It is one of the best-kept secrets of all time. No one knows who all was there.

KIMIKO: Now that sounds interesting. It's hard to keep a secret. Tell me more. Why did they destroy the tea? Didn't they like tea?

GRANDMA: *(laughs)* Yes, they liked tea, but they didn't want to have to pay a tea tax.

KIMIKO: But everybody has to pay taxes.

GRANDMA: Yes, but the difference is today we elect the people who make the laws for things like taxes. We have a say in how things are done, but the colonists did not have a say. They did not like "taxation without representation."

KIMIKO: So there were no colonists in **Parliament**?

GRANDMA: Right, the members of Parliament represented the people of England. But the people in the colonies were not allowed to have someone represent them in Parliament.

KIMIKO: I bet the colonists didn't like that.

GRANDMA: They didn't. But when England needed money, Parliament decided the colonists should pay taxes on tea. Everyone drank tea, so everyone would pay the tax. England decided only one company could bring tea to America, and only special merchants could sell the tea.

PAUL REVERE: *(holding up sign that says "Boston, 1773")* News has come from New York and Philadelphia. A group calling itself "The Mohawks" sent a letter to each merchant. It said that anyone who helped with the tea would receive an "unwelcome visit" from the Mohawks.

A Boston Teapot
Readers' Theater 5, SV 9781419031700

SAMUEL ADAMS: Without tea merchants, there will be no one to receive or sell the tea.

PAUL REVERE: Yes, so the cities are refusing any **shipments** of tea.

SAMUEL ADAMS: We must convince our tea merchants in Boston to do the same.

DR. YOUNG: That won't be easy. Two of our merchants are sons of the governor. Governor Hutchinson is **loyal** to England.

KIMIKO: Let me guess. The colonists couldn't convince the Boston tea merchants, right?

GRANDMA: No, they couldn't. So the colonists decided to resist and return any shipments of tea.

(Paul Revere holds sign saying "November 28, 1773.")

SAMUEL ADAMS: *(writing a letter)* We must join forces. We must **unite** to resist England. England has given us only one choice. We can choose to be slaves of England and accept the tea and the unfair tax. Or we can resist like free people.

FLUENCY TIP

Make sure you know how to pronounce the names of the places in this play. Use a dictionary to help you.

PAUL REVERE: *(running in)* The moment of truth has come. A tea ship named the *Dartmouth* has entered the harbor.

SAMUEL ADAMS: We can't let them unload the tea.

PAUL REVERE: We can put off the unloading for twenty days. Then the officers will step in and force the unloading.

SAMUEL ADAMS: We'll need guards on the *Dartmouth*. Get 25 **volunteers** to board the ship each evening. They must prevent any attempt to bring the tea on land.

DR. YOUNG: Yes, and send your letter with the fastest riders. Let's have a meeting as soon as possible.

(Paul Revere holds sign saying "Special Town Meeting.")

SAMUEL ADAMS: *(speaking to crowd of thousands)* We must stop the unloading of the ship. We must refuse to pay the tax. We must not give in to England!

CROWD: *(cheering)* Yes! Yes!

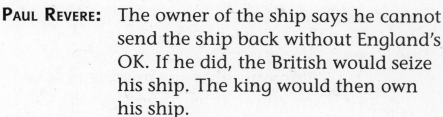

PAUL REVERE: The owner of the ship says he cannot send the ship back without England's OK. If he did, the British would seize his ship. The king would then own his ship.

DR. YOUNG: There may be only one way to get rid of the tea. We may have to dump it overboard.

CROWD: Yes!

SAMUEL ADAMS: We must try to return the tea first.

GRANDMA: For the next 16 days, the colonists tried everything they could to return the tea to England. During that time, two more tea ships arrived.

KIMIKO: They were running out of time.

GRANDMA: Yes. They must have been planning the "tea party." On the evening of December 16, 1773, there was another town meeting.

(Paul Revere holds sign saying "Special Town Meeting.")

PAUL REVERE: If nothing is done, tomorrow the officers will seize the tea and bring it on land. The tax then must be paid.

DR. YOUNG: I wonder how tea mixes with salt water.

Readers' Theater 5, SV 9781419031700

CROWD: Yes!

PAUL REVERE: We must not be seen as a mob. We must not hurt anyone or take anything other than the tea.

CROWD: Boston Harbor a teapot tonight! The Mohawks are coming!

GRANDMA: Suddenly the meeting was over, and a crowd was headed to the **wharf**. Some were disguised as Mohawks and were carrying hatchets.

KIMIKO: My book says they chopped open the tea chests. Then they dumped the tea into the sea.

SAMUEL ADAMS: No one must ever know who was at the tea party. They could hang for this.

DR. YOUNG: Let us think of happier thoughts tonight. Look, the job is nearly done. The crowd is breaking up and going home. A little tea was spilled. That is all.

SAMUEL ADAMS: Yes, but who knows what happens next because of this tea party?

FLUENCY TIP

Don't skip any words. If you did, look them up now since you have read the whole play.

Comprehension

Write your answer to each question on the lines below.

1. Why do the colonists refuse to pay the tax on tea?

_____

_____

2. Why do some participants in the Boston Tea Party disguise themselves?

_____

_____

3. What does "taxation without representation" mean?

_____

_____

4. Why do you think the colonists first try to return the tea to England?

_____

_____

5. Whose side are you on? Parliament's or the colonists? Why?

_____

_____

6. What is one answer to Samuel Adams's question: ". . . what happens next because of this tea party?"

_____

_____

7. What event in the play reminds you of something in your life?

_____

_____

Readers' Theater 5, SV 9781419031700

Vocabulary

Write the number of a vocabulary word on the line before its meaning.

1. unite   _____ Place where ships unload

2. loyal   _____ Goods sent by ship, train, or mail

3. shipment   _____ One who offers to do something

4. wharf   _____ True to another

5. disguised   _____ Come together for a purpose

6. volunteer   _____ Lawmaking body of England

7. Parliament   _____ Wearing a costume

Extension

1. What would you have done if you were living in Boston at the time of the Boston Tea Party? With a partner, discuss what each of you would have done and why.

   - Would you have gone to the town meetings?

   - Would you have taken part in the "tea party"?

   - Would you have watched?

2. With a partner, do some research on what it was like to live in Boston in the 1770s. What kinds of jobs did people have? What did they wear? What did they eat? Present your findings to the class.

     Readers' Theater 5, SV 9781419031700

The Railroad Race

Summary

"The Railroad Race" is a six-character play about the role of immigrants in building the transcontinental railroad.

Meet the Players

Character	Reading Level
Central Pacific Narrator	7.9
Union Pacific Narrator	8.1
Irish Worker Pat	4.3
Irish Worker Ian	3.6
Chinese Worker Lok	2.8
Chinese Worker Chen	2.1

Fluency Focus
Reading with Word Accuracy

Comprehension Focus
Making Connections

Vocabulary
congratulations
immigrant
ledge
spectacular
surveyor
telegraph
tough
transcontinental

Read Aloud Tip

Introduce the fluency focus of **reading with word accuracy**. Point out that a fluent reader reads every word without skipping any. Ask students to listen carefully as you read aloud, raising their hands if something does not make sense. As you read, skip an occasional word. Then correct the error by rereading the sentence accurately, inviting students to read along with you.

Set the Stage

Teacher Read Aloud page 73

This selection is about the settlement of California during the 1800s. Read the selection aloud. As you do, model good fluency by reading each word clearly and accurately.

Get Ready

Vocabulary page 74

Use this page to introduce vocabulary. Discuss the Vocabulary Think Tank question, challenging each student to give two reasons why his or her example is spectacular.

Fluency and Comprehension Warm-Ups pages 74–75

Review these pages with students. Use the following for students who need additional help with the concepts:

- **Reading with Word Accuracy** When you come to unfamiliar words, remember to look for parts of the word that you do know. Put the parts together to say a word that makes sense. Then practice saying the word. Try doing this with a word from the Read Aloud, such as *continent*.

- **Making Connections** When you make connections, you link the text to something you have read before, to your own experiences, or to something that has happened in the world. What connections can you make between the Read Aloud and other texts you have read about the United States during the 1800s?

The Railroad Race *pages 76–82*

Independent Practice

Set up the groups and assign each student a part. Then have students read through their assigned parts once before small group practice begins.

Small Group Practice

Assemble the groups. You may want to use the following rehearsal schedule. Each rehearsal, which should involve a complete oral read-through, has an activity to guide students.

1. First Rehearsal: Challenge students to preview the play and to create a T-Chart that names the two railroads, tells the direction each was headed, and tells which immigrant group worked for each railroad. Then invite students to read together. Use the T-Chart on page 11.

2. Vocabulary Rehearsal: Have students locate the play's vocabulary words. As students locate each word, ask them to read in unison the sentence that includes that word. Challenge volunteers to use the words in sentences that explain the word's meaning, such as *Immigrants are people who come to a new country to live.*

3. Fluency Rehearsal: Reading with Word Accuracy Have one student in each group read aloud the tip on page 77. Then invite students to survey the play to locate and list names of places. Ask groups to work together to clarify how each place name is pronounced.

4. Comprehension Rehearsal: Making Connections Ask students to think about connections they can make between this play and their own experiences. Then have them answer the questions below.

- How does this play remind us of other plays or stories we have read?
- How does the modern achievement of sending people into space compare to that of building the transcontinental railroad?

5. Final Rehearsal: Observe this rehearsal, focusing on how each student reads with word accuracy. For example, do the narrators accurately read the names of people and places in their lines?

Performance

This is your opportunity to sit back, relax, and enjoy the performance. Encourage students to have fun while performing!

Curtain Call *pages 83–84*

Assign these questions and activities for students to complete in a group or independently.

Vocabulary Tip

For more vocabulary practice, have students discuss the following:

- Name an occasion when you might say "**congratulations!**"
- How might **ledges** be helpful to mountain climbers?
- What is one thing that you find **tough** to do?

The Railroad Race
Readers' Theater 5, SV 9781419031700

The Railroad Race

Set the Stage
Teacher Read Aloud

In 1848, gold was discovered in California. The rush to California began early in 1849. Some people from the East Coast sailed around South America to California—a journey of 18,000 miles. However, most gold seekers from the East traveled across the continent. This was a journey of 2,000 miles, and it took 4 to 6 months. Travelers had to cross plains, mountains, and deserts.

Americans were not the only ones rushing to California. Many immigrants came from countries such as China. Most of these immigrants arrived in San Francisco. The population of San Francisco went from just 600 in 1848 to 25,000 in 1849!

California became a state in 1850. In 1860, President Abraham Lincoln worried that California, like the South, might be thinking about breaking away from the Union. He wanted a way to hold the country together. The transcontinental railroad would provide that vital link between California and other states.

In this play, you will learn about the building of the first transcontinental railroad. Use the vocabulary and warm-ups to help you get ready.

Get Ready

Vocabulary

Read and review these vocabulary words to prepare you for reading this play. Say these words to yourself. Then say them each aloud two times.

congratulations—an expression of happiness for a job well done

immigrant—a person who leaves one country to live in another

ledge—a cut on a cliff or rock wall forming a shelf

spectacular—very wonderful

surveyor—a person who studies the land to plan how to build on it

telegraph—a way of communicating before the telephone

tough—very difficult

transcontinental—crossing the continent

> **VOCABULARY THINK TANK**
>
> Have you ever seen something you would describe as spectacular? Explain.

Fluency Warm-Up

Reading with Word Accuracy

To read fluently and smoothly, you need to read all of the words with **accuracy**. Fluent readers learn all the words in a story. They learn how to pronounce the words, and they learn what the words mean.

Remember to learn how to pronounce difficult words, names of people, and names of places. Do not skip words. Practice so you can read smoothly.

> **FLUENCY PRACTICE**
>
> Practice reading aloud the underlined words below. Then read each complete sentence aloud smoothly.
>
> 1. The Union Pacific was a railroad.
> 2. The transcontinental railroad started in Omaha, Nebraska.
> 3. It ended in Sacramento, California.

The Railroad Race
Readers' Theater 5, SV 9781419031700

Comprehension Warm-Up

Making Connections

When you think about how one story reminds you of another story, you are **making connections**. You can make connections in other ways, too.

You can connect something you've read to another book. You can connect something you've read to your own life. Or you can connect something you've read to something that has happened in the world.

COMPREHENSION TIP

As you read, ask yourself questions like these.

1. How does this story remind me of other stories I've read?
2. How does my life compare to this character's life?
3. How do the events in this story fit with what I know of the world?

Readers' Theater

Presents
The Railroad Race
by
Carol M. Elliott

Cast
(in order of appearance)

Central Pacific Narrator _____

Union Pacific Narrator _____

Irish Worker Pat _____

Irish Worker Ian _____

Chinese Worker Lok _____

Chinese Worker Chen _____

CP NARRATOR: President Abraham Lincoln knew a railroad was needed to bind the country together.

UP NARRATOR: Therefore, in 1862 President Lincoln authorized the building of the **transcontinental** railroad. It would connect the railroads in the East to California.

CP NARRATOR: To speed up the building of the railroad, two companies were selected to start at opposite ends. The Central Pacific would start in Sacramento, California, and build east.

UP NARRATOR: The company that built more miles of track would get more money. It was a race.

CP NARRATOR: The Central Pacific had it **tough**. Every length of track and every tool needed to build a railroad had to come from the East. Ships carrying the supplies had to sail all the way around South America to get to California.

FLUENCY TIP

Practice pronouncing the names of the places in this play before you go on.

Readers' Theater 5, SV 9781419031700

UP Narrator: It wasn't easy at first for the Union Pacific either. The eastern United States was fighting the Civil War. Many men were soldiers.

CP Narrator: The **surveyors** for the Central Pacific faced a real challenge. They had to figure out how to get through the Sierra Nevada Mountains.

UP Narrator: In 1865, the Civil War ended. The Union Pacific needed thousands of workers. The company hired many soldiers. It also hired many Irish **immigrants**.

Irish Worker Pat: *(making shoveling motion)* All day we shovel and haul dirt. I wish we could just lay the track on the ground.

Irish Worker Ian: *(making hand motions to go with description)* You know we can't do that. The tracks have to be level. Every rise in the land has to be cut through. Every dip filled in. The roadbed has to be at least a few feet above the ground. That keeps spring floods from washing away the track.

Irish Worker Pat: Why are we building this railroad out here anyway? Nobody lives out here but the Sioux and the Cheyenne.

Readers' Theater 5, SV 9781419031700

IRISH WORKER IAN: There will be people living out here before long. You wait and see. Towns will be built wherever the train goes.

IRISH WORKER PAT: Yes. Well then, hurry up and shovel. This is a race that the Union Pacific needs to win.

CP NARRATOR: Although the Central Pacific had started in 1863, it didn't get too far until 1865. The company couldn't get enough good workers until it decided to hire Chinese immigrants. The Chinese proved to be very good workers. By the end of 1865, the Central Pacific had hired thousands of Chinese.

CHINESE WORKER LOK: *(making a cutting hand motion)* The company wants to cut a **ledge** in the side of that mountain. It wants the tracks to curve around the mountain.

CHINESE WORKER CHEN: *(pointing upward on the word* steep*)* That will be tough. The side of the mountain is very steep. And the rock is very hard.

CHINESE WORKER LOK: We will need lots of black powder and fuses to blow away the rock.

Readers' Theater 5, SV 9781419031700

CHINESE WORKER CHEN: There isn't any place for men to stand and work. And there isn't any place to run once the fuses have been lit.

CHINESE WORKER LOK: We will need to lower the men on ropes from above. We can tie the ropes to trees to be safe.

CHINESE WORKER CHEN: Yes, that could work. The men will drill holes into the cliff. They will fill the holes with black powder and light the fuse. Then they'll have to get away!

CHINESE WORKER LOK: *(pretends to be afraid)* We will need men who are not scared of heights. Tell them not to look down!

UP NARRATOR: On the Union Pacific side, there were thousands of railroad workers to be fed. Men were hired to hunt buffalo for meat for the railroad workers. The Sioux and the Cheyenne did not like what was happening.

IRISH WORKER PAT: Did you hear? There's been another attack by the Sioux and the Cheyenne. Isn't there enough land here for us and them?

IRISH WORKER IAN: I don't know. I hear the buffalo won't cross the tracks. That's why we've been eating so much buffalo meat lately.

CP Narrator: In the fall of 1866, Chinese workers were digging seven long tunnels through the mountains. They worked all winter inside the tunnels.

Chinese Worker Lok: *(wiping sweat from his brow, exhausted)* Every day we drill holes by hand and blast away at this tunnel. We can only get about a foot done each day.

Chinese Worker Chen: Crews are working around the clock.

Chinese Worker Lok: I heard that crews are working at both ends of the tunnel. What if the tunnels aren't dug right, and the two ends don't meet?

Chinese Worker Chen *(with confidence)* They will meet. We are Chinese, and we will do it right!

CP Narrator: In August 1867, there was a blast in one of the tunnels. When the smoke cleared, the Chinese workers felt a fresh breeze. They had finally broken through! Meanwhile, out in the Nevada desert, the workers were laying track as fast as they could.

FLUENCY TIP

Make a list of any words that are difficult to pronounce. Practice reading them aloud.

The Railroad Race
Readers' Theater 5, SV 9781419031700

IRISH WORKER PAT: Can you believe it? The Central Pacific laid more than six miles of track in one day!

IRISH WORKER IAN: We can beat that!

IRISH WORKER PAT: We don't need to. The Union Pacific is way ahead in this race.

CP NARRATOR: Finally in 1869, the two companies agreed that the meeting point would be at Promontory Summit, Utah.

UP NARRATOR: On May 10, 1869, crowds gathered in Promontory Summit. **Telegraph** wires had been strung along the tracks as each part of the railroad was built. They were now connected to make a transcontinental telegraph line.

CP NARRATOR: The workers laid the final tracks. The final spike was made of gold. The first message to be telegraphed across the entire country was the word "Done!"

IRISH WORKERS: We have done something **spectacular**!

CHINESE WORKERS: We have done what many thought was impossible!

ALL WORKERS: **Congratulations**! It is done.

> **FLUENCY TIP**
>
> If you skipped any words, find them and write them down. Now practice reading them aloud.

Comprehension

Write your answer to each question on the lines below.

1. What were two dangers faced by workers on the transcontinental railroad? _____

_____

2. Why were the Native Americans upset about the railroad?

_____

_____

3. Why did the workers have to build the roadbed higher than the ground?

_____

_____

4. Why do you think the final railroad spike was made of gold?

_____

_____

5. Name a book you have read that is about someone changing the United States. If you can't think of a book, explain how you would find one.

_____

_____

6. What reasons were given to explain why the transcontinental railroad was built? _____

_____

7. What is your experience with trains? Tell a story.

_____

_____

Vocabulary

Write the vocabulary word that answers the question.

> spectacular   immigrant   congratulations   ledge
> surveyor   transcontinental   telegraph   tough

1. Which word means "across the continent"? _____

2. Which word names an invention that improved communication?

   _____

3. Which word names a person who plans where roads go? _____

4. Which word means the opposite of *easy*? _____

5. Which word is a synonym for *astounding*? _____

Extension

1. What would you have done if you were living at the time the transcontinental railroad was being built? With a partner, discuss what you would have done and why.
   - Would you have wanted to work on the railroad? Why or why not?
   - Would you have wanted to ride on the transcontinental railroad? Why or why not?

   Trace the route of the transcontinental railroad on the map on page 12.

2. With a partner, write and give an oral report comparing a method of travel in the 1800s to a method today. For example,
   - a horse and wagon—to a minivan,
   - a Mississippi steamboat—to a cruise ship, or
   - the transcontinental railroad—to a modern passenger train.

   Use the Venn Diagram on page 13.

The Hills Are Alive

Summary

"The Hills Are Alive" is a six-character play about Mount Rushmore's presidents, who mysteriously leave the monument to learn about modern life.

Meet the Players

Character	Reading Level
Kim	4.1
Lin	2.4
George Washington	3.8
Abraham Lincoln	4.6
Thomas Jefferson	3.4
Teddy Roosevelt	5.5

Fluency Focus
Using Punctuation

Comprehension Focus
Making Inferences

Vocabulary
admire
declare/declaration
extraordinary
leeches
legacy
memorial
nickname
portrait

Read Aloud Tip

Introduce the fluency focus: **using punctuation**. Direct students' attention to the first sentence in the final paragraph and ask them to identify the punctuation marks. Then reread the sentence. Have students listen as you pause at the comma and use an excited voice to reflect the exclamation point. Invite students to join in on a second rereading.

Set the Stage

Teacher Read Aloud *page 87*
This selection is about Mount Rushmore. Read the selection aloud, pausing at commas and making full stops at the ends of sentences.

Get Ready

Vocabulary *page 88*
Use this page to introduce vocabulary. Discuss the Vocabulary Think Tank question, asking students to share any special Memorial Day experiences.

Fluency and Comprehension Warm-Ups *pages 88–89*
Review these pages with students. Use the following for students who need additional help with the concepts:

• **Using Punctuation** When you read aloud, don't rush. Come to a full stop at the end of every sentence—even short ones. Try reading the last three sentences in paragraph 1, stopping at the periods.

• **Making Inferences** An inference is a sensible guess you make about something that is not stated directly in the text. After reading this selection, you may have inferred that creating Mount Rushmore was expensive. This makes sense because the author says the project had financial delays.

Readers' Theater 5, SV 9781419031700

The Hills Are Alive *pages 90–96*

Independent Practice

Set up the groups and assign each student a part. Then have students read through their assigned parts once before small group practice begins.

Small Group Practice

Assemble the groups. You may want to use the following rehearsal schedule. Each rehearsal, which should involve a complete oral read-through, has an activity to guide students.

1. First Rehearsal: Point out that this play includes many stage directions. Encourage students to locate and practice a stage direction for their characters. Then invite students to read together for the first time.

2. Vocabulary Rehearsal: Have students locate and list the vocabulary words used in the play. Challenge groups to work together to choose one word and to create a Word Web by writing the word at the center of the Word Web on page 14 and surrounding it with ideas associated with that word.

3. Fluency Rehearsal: Using Punctuation During the rehearsal, ask students to note question marks and exclamation points in their lines and to read these lines in an appropriate tone of voice. After the rehearsal, invite volunteers to choose one question or exclamation to read aloud to the group.

4. Comprehension Rehearsal: Making Inferences Write the questions below on the board. Ask students to look for clues as they read to help them infer the answers. Then have groups work together to write the answers.

- What might happen if the presidents don't return to the monument?
- What does Abraham Lincoln mean when he says that Kim and Lin "live in a rich time"?

5. Final Rehearsal: Observe this rehearsal, focusing on students' use of punctuation. For example, when Lin reads her lines on page 91, does the student pause at each comma?

Performance

This is your opportunity to sit back, relax, and enjoy the performance. Encourage students to have fun while performing!

Curtain Call *pages 97–98*

Assign these questions and activities for students to complete independently or in a group.

Vocabulary Tip

For more vocabulary practice, have students discuss the following:

- Name someone you **admire**, and explain why you admire him or her.

- What is the most **extraordinary** experience you have ever had?

- How is a family tradition a **legacy**?

The Hills Are Alive

Set the Stage

Teacher Read Aloud

Mount Rushmore is a national memorial in South Dakota. The faces of four great U.S. presidents are carved into the mountain. George Washington is there as a memorial for his part in gaining independence from England. Thomas Jefferson declared that the government should be for the people and by the people. Jefferson wrote the Declaration of Independence. Abraham Lincoln is honored for his work toward equality. He freed the slaves. Theodore Roosevelt is recognized for his role in world politics. He sought to make the United States one of the world's great powers.

Each face on Mount Rushmore is 465 feet high. The carvings took 14 years to complete because of bad weather and financial delays. The monument was finished in 1941.

Mount Rushmore is considered by many to be the world's greatest mountain carving.

In this play, you will read about what might happen if the presidents on Mount Rushmore could come back to life! Use the vocabulary and warm-ups to help you get ready.

Vocabulary

Review these vocabulary words to prepare you for reading this play. Pick the word that you find most interesting and tell a friend.

admire—to appreciate greatly for fine qualities

declare/declaration—to make known; a document

extraordinary—beyond what is common and usual

leeches—blood-sucking worms used as a medical treatment long ago

legacy—something handed down to other generations

memorial—a reminder of an event or person

nickname—a name used instead of an official name

portrait—a picture of a person

> **VOCABULARY THINK TANK**
>
> Memorial Day is a special holiday at the end of May. What is the purpose of Memorial Day?

Fluency Warm-Up

Using Punctuation

Fluent readers pay attention to **punctuation**. They know where the punctuation is and what it stands for. You need to change the way you read based on the punctuation.

When you get to a punctuation mark, don't skip it and race forward. Stop at periods. Pause at commas. Use your question voice at a question mark. Express excitement at an exclamation point.

> **FLUENCY PRACTICE**
>
> Read the sentences aloud. Watch the punctuation.
>
> 1. I went to the store, bought some eggs, and ran home. Oops!
> 2. Did I ask him to bring a dollar?
> 3. "Hurry up!" he shouted.

Comprehension Warm-Up

Making Inferences

An **inference** is an educated guess that you make about your reading. To make an inference, use clues in the reading and your own experience.

One way to practice making inferences is to ask yourself questions as you read. Then you can use what you know to figure out the best answers.

COMPREHENSION TIP

Ask questions like these as you read.

- What kind of person is this character?
- Why did the author write this way?
- What will happen next?

Readers' Theater

Presents
The Hills Are Alive
by
Laura Layton Strom

Cast
(in order of appearance)

Kim   _____

Lin   _____

George Washington   _____

Abraham Lincoln   _____

Thomas Jefferson   _____

Teddy Roosevelt   _____

The Hills Are Alive
Readers' Theater 5, SV 9781419031700

KIM: *(clicking off car radio)* Hey, Lin. Did you just hear that? The radio announcer said there were strange lights spotted over Mount Rushmore tonight.

LIN: *(getting out of car and looking up)* Yes, and this mall parking lot is just down the hill from the monument. I don't see any strange lights right now. The park is closed this week for improvements, so everything should be dark.

KIM: *(pointing toward the mall)* Look at those four unusual-looking men. They are standing outside Iron's Department Store. Nice costumes. I wonder what they are selling. Let's check them out!

GEORGE: Excuse me, ladies. So sorry to bother you. Might my friends and I have a word with you?

KIM: *(pulls a dollar bill from her purse)* Look, all I have is a dollar, so I can't buy whatever you are selling.

GEORGE: Hmm. That paper has my picture on it. How odd. Anyway, I am not selling anything, dear ladies. Please allow me to introduce myself. My name is George. George Washington. These are my friends Abraham, Thomas, and Teddy.

ABRAHAM: *(extending his hand)* Abraham Lincoln. It is a pleasure.

THOMAS: *(shyly)* Um, Thomas, um, Jefferson. Hello.

TEDDY: *(big handshake)* Well, hello there, young ladies. Theodore Roosevelt here. Teddy is my **nickname**.

KIM AND LIN: *(rolling eyes, unbelieving and in unison)* Right.

THOMAS: I'm sure this is a surprise for you. Believe me, we were quite surprised as well. I was used to being a stone face.

ABRAHAM: Our faces have been up on that mountain for over sixty years. But something strange happened tonight.

FLUENCY TIP

Sometimes people don't speak in complete sentences. Stop and take a breath at periods, even if the sentence is a fragment.

Readers' Theater 5, SV 9781419031700

George: We are not really sure what occurred. There were bright, hot lights, and then we were like this. *(Pointing down his body.)* But we have a feeling this effect on our persons will last only a short time. I do not think the park service would like it if the Mount Rushmore faces went missing!

Teddy: So, we were quite hoping you might show us what life is like during your time. I'm sure there are new, **extraordinary** things you can share.

Kim: We would be honored to show you around. We know your story must be true because we learned in school that you don't lie, Mr. Washington.

George: Ah, yes. A charming tale was told about that cherry tree. But it is true that I despise lying.

Kim: *(looking at the mall directory)* Hmm. I wonder where we should go first.

Lin: *(pointing)* Hey, Mr. Roosevelt. I bet you'd like this store. It's called "My Teddy." It's a store where people create their own teddy bears.

Teddy: Ha! Who would have thought that rescuing an innocent cub would have led to a stuffed bear shop in the twenty-first century!

The Hills Are Alive
Readers' Theater 5, SV 9781419031700

KIM: The electronics store would be interesting to all of you. We can show you TVs that show live events from around the world as they happen. We have computers with e-mail. E-mail lets us write letters and send them all over the world in seconds!

THOMAS: I was very fond of writing letters in my day. When I worked in France, my children lived in the United States. E-mail would have given me more letters from my children.

ABRAHAM: You were a magnificent writer, Thomas. I especially like the **Declaration** of Independence. I spent a great portion of my time writing, too. And I read constantly.

THOMAS: I sometimes read for 15 hours at one sitting. Some people called me a bookworm.

LIN: Well then, we should definitely go to a bookstore. They have tons of books.

ABRAHAM: You live in a rich time. I envy that. Your blessings are great.

KIM: Before we start our shopping, let's go to the food court. I'm hungry!

(Lin buys everyone hamburgers and fries.)

The Hills Are Alive
Readers' Theater 5, SV 9781419031700

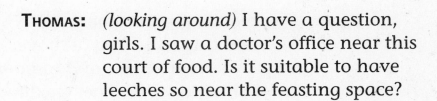

THOMAS: *(looking around)* I have a question, girls. I saw a doctor's office near this court of food. Is it suitable to have leeches so near the feasting space?

KIM: Oh, we don't use **leeches** anymore, Mr. Jefferson. We use pills and other medicines.

GEORGE: So, they learned leeches are not the answer, eh? Well, I guess I am finding that out a bit late. Before I died, I was treated with leeches.

LIN: Let's go to the bookstore now. I got some cash at the ATM so you could each buy a book. Here you go. *(Hands them cash.)*

ABRAHAM: Look! My portrait is on this five-dollar bill. *(Kidding around.)* I guess I am more **admired** than you are, George.

GEORGE: But I am on the twenty-five-cent piece, too. You got the lousy one-cent piece.

ABRAHAM: Well, you've got me there. I can't compete on coins!

> **FLUENCY TIP**
>
> Notice the commas on this page. Make sure you are pausing at the commas.

TEDDY: I picked the **portrait** for that one-cent coin, Abe. You all have your own monuments and **memorials** in Washington, D.C. I get a stuffed bear store as my **legacy**!

(Presidents all laugh.)

KIM: It is getting late, and it is time for the mall to close.

THOMAS: Thank you for the tour. Thank you so much for the food and books, too.

LIN: You are so welcome. This is a treat for us, too. It isn't every day we get to grab burgers and shop with four presidents!

(The next morning arrives.)

KIM: Good morning, Lin. Did you hear the news yet? *(Lin shakes her head no.)* Mount Rushmore reopened this morning. When they took the cloth covering off the stone faces, some strange things popped out. They found books about the four presidents, a one-dollar bill, a five-dollar bill, and some coins. No one knows exactly why.

LIN: *(winking at her sister)* Yeah. NO ONE knows!

> **FLUENCY TIP**
>
> On this page, there is a question mark and several exclamation points. Reread this page, emphasizing the punctuation shown.

The Hills Are Alive
Readers' Theater 5, SV 9781419031700

Comprehension

Write your answer to each question on the lines below.

1. Why does Kim pull a dollar bill out of her purse?

   _____

   _____

2. When the presidents introduce themselves, what do Kim and Lin think?

   _____

   _____

3. Why does George Washington call the cherry tree story a "charming

   tale"? _____

   _____

4. Name at least two things that each of the four presidents is famous for.

   _____

   _____

5. What do the presidents learn about leeches?

   _____

   _____

6. Why are there books, dollars, and coins under the cloth covering at

   Mount Rushmore? _____

   _____

7. How do you think the presidents came to life? Use your imagination to

   answer! _____

   _____

Vocabulary

Write each vocabulary word on the line where it belongs.

leeches	nickname	declaration	extraordinary
portrait	admire	legacy	Memorial

1. Doctors once thought that using _____ to drain blood would help a patient get better.

2. We visited the Lincoln _____ in Washington, D.C.

3. Before cameras were invented, a _____ showed what a person looked like.

4. Washington, Lincoln, and Roosevelt are each remembered for doing a(n) _____ job as president.

5. Abraham Lincoln's _____ was "Honest Abe."

Extension

1. With a partner, discuss how you would have reacted if you were approached by the four Mount Rushmore presidents.

   • Would you have reacted like Kim and Lin?

   • Would you have shown the presidents around the mall?

   • Would you have taken them somewhere else? If so, where?

2. With a partner, do some research on a recent or current president. On index cards, write six trivia questions about him. Then take turns quizzing the class and reading the answers.

It's a Capital Idea!

Summary

"It's a Capital Idea!" is a six-character play about a group of students who are touring the nation's capital.

Meet the Players

Character	Reading Level
Tour Guide	5.8
Denzel	6.3
Jen	3.8
Roberto	2.5
Peter	7.9
Lila	4.8

Fluency Focus
Phrasing Properly

Comprehension Focus
Monitoring Comprehension

Vocabulary
architect
capital
Capitol
forefathers
memorial
monument

Read Aloud Tip

Introduce the fluency focus of **phrasing properly**. Write the second sentence in paragraph 4 on the board. Ask students to listen to how you chunk, or group, the words as you read the sentence aloud. Explain that the commas helped you decide how to chunk the words. Then draw lines to show the proper phrasing of the sentence. Invite students to reread the sentence with you.

Set the Stage

Teacher Read Aloud   *page 101*

This selection is about the planning of the U.S. Capitol in Washington, D.C. Read the selection aloud. As you do, model good fluency, slightly exaggerating your phrasing.

Get Ready

Vocabulary   *page 102*

Use this page to introduce vocabulary. Discuss the Vocabulary Think Tank question. Have students locate their state capital on a map.

Fluency and Comprehension Warm-Ups   *pages 102–103*

Review these pages with students. Use the following for students who need additional help with the concepts:

- **Phrasing Properly** Listen to this phrasing of the first sentence of paragraph 2: *It was George—Washington—who chose this site for the—new capital.* Now listen to this: *It was George Washington—who chose this site—for the new capital.* Which one makes more sense? The second example chunks words in a way that makes sense. Try reading this sentence both ways aloud.

- **Monitoring Comprehension** Checking to make sure that what you are reading makes sense is called monitoring comprehension. If you mispronounced or skipped a word, the sentence may not make sense. Listen to this sentence from the Read Aloud: *Pigs and chickens freely.* Does the sentence make sense? Why not?

www.harcourtschoolsupply.com
© Harcourt Achieve Inc. All rights reserved.

99

It's a Capital Idea!
Readers' Theater 5, SV 9781419031700

It's a Capital Idea! *pages 104–110*

Independent Practice

Set up the groups and assign each student a part. Then have students read through their assigned parts once before small group practice begins.

Small Group Practice

Assemble the groups. You may want to use the following rehearsal schedule. Each rehearsal, which should involve a complete oral read-through, has an activity to guide students.

1. First Rehearsal:
Ask students to preview the play to list at least three places the characters visit while in Washington, D.C. Then invite them to read together as a group for the first time.

2. Vocabulary Rehearsal:
Before this rehearsal, ask students to locate and list vocabulary words used in the play. Have them alternate reading aloud sentences that include the words.

3. Fluency Rehearsal: Phrasing Properly
Review the fluency instruction on page 102. Then appoint one student as the tip reader. This student will stop the rehearsal to read aloud Fluency Tips as they appear in the play. After the rehearsal, have students take turns rereading the tips and applying each tip by reading aloud an appropriate line from the play.

4. Comprehension Rehearsal: Monitoring Comprehension
Before this rehearsal, encourage groups to reread the Comprehension Tips on page 103. Then ask them to carefully monitor their reading during this rehearsal, stopping to fix problems as they arise. After reading, have groups write one or two sentences that answer the question "What is the author's main point?"

5. Final Rehearsal:
Observe this rehearsal, focusing on students' phrasing. For example, when Roberto reads his first line, does the student read the incomplete sentence as a chunk?

Performance

This is your opportunity to sit back, relax, and enjoy the performance. Encourage students to have fun while performing!

Curtain Call *pages 111–112*

Assign these questions and activities for students to complete in a group or independently.

Vocabulary Tip

For more vocabulary practice, have students discuss the following:

- Do all people have **forefathers**? Why or why not?

- How are **memorials** and **monuments** the same?

- When might you hire an **architect**?

Readers' Theater 5, SV 9781419031700

Set the Stage
Teacher Read Aloud

The Washington, D.C., of today looks very different than it did in the late 1700s. At that time, the site of the future capital of the United States was a swampy piece of land on the Potomac River. There were only two unpaved streets, and most of the houses were small shacks. Pigs and chickens roamed freely.

It was George Washington who chose this site for the new capital. He also chose the man he wanted to plan the new capital— Pierre Charles L'Enfant (lawn FAWN). L'Enfant came to America from France in 1776 to fight in the American Revolution. Like Washington, he believed in the ideals of freedom and equality.

Unfortunately, L'Enfant had trouble getting along with people. Washington had to fire L'Enfant, who returned to France and took his brilliant plans for the capital city with him!

Two men on L'Enfant's planning commission saved the day—and the new capital! Andrew Ellicott, a surveyor, and his assistant, Benjamin Banneker, an African American scientist and mathematician, had both taken pages and pages of notes detailing L'Enfant's plan. What wasn't written in the notes, Banneker had memorized!

Today the capital of the United States exists much as L'Enfant envisioned it. It is a beautiful, bustling city. It's the home of the U.S. president. It's the home of all major offices of the federal government. And it's a symbol of freedom and equality for all the world to see.

In this play, you will learn more about the nation's capital. Use the vocabulary and warm-ups to help you get ready.

Vocabulary

Read these vocabulary words aloud with a partner. These words will help prepare you for reading this play.

architect—a person who designs buildings

capital—the city where the government of a country or state is located

Capitol—the building that is home to the United States Congress

forefathers—ancestors

memorial—a building or statue to honor an important person or event from the past

monument—an object built in memory of a person, deed, or special event

> **VOCABULARY THINK TANK**
>
> What is your state's capital? Where is it?

Fluency Warm-Up

Phrasing Properly

Fluent readers read in chunks, or **phrases**. Phrasing properly is important if you want to read with fluency. When you read word-for-word, you may not understand the meaning of a sentence. Also, what you read will be boring!

Punctuation will help you phrase properly. However, sometimes you won't be able to rely on punctuation. Be sure to listen to yourself as you read aloud. Chunk words together into phrases that make sense together. If a sentence doesn't make sense, try chunking it differently.

> **FLUENCY PRACTICE**
>
> Chunk this sentence into phrases. Is there more than one way to read this sentence?
>
> The U.S. White House has 132 rooms, including 3 kitchens and 32 bathrooms.

It's a Capital Idea!
Readers' Theater 5, SV 9781419031700

Comprehension Warm-Up

Monitoring Comprehension

When you **monitor comprehension**, you check to make sure that what you are reading makes sense.

Good readers realize when they do not understand something, and then they fix it! They use strategies to understand. They try to get more information to help them. Understanding makes reading more enjoyable!

COMPREHENSION TIP

As you read, ask yourself questions like the ones below. Then use clues in the reading to help you figure out the answers.

- Do I know the meaning of this word?
- Does this sentence make sense to me?
- How does this sentence fit with the others?
- What is the author's main point?

103
It's a Capital Idea!
Readers' Theater 5, SV 9781419031700

Readers' Theater

Presents
It's a Capital Idea!
by
Natalie West and Loretta West

Cast
(in order of appearance)

Tour Guide _____

Denzel _____

Jen _____

Roberto _____

Peter _____

Lila _____

www.harcourtschoolsupply.com

104

It's a Capital Idea!
Readers' Theater 5, SV 9781419031700

TOUR GUIDE: Welcome to Washington, D.C.! I'll be your tour guide for the next three days. It's a great honor for me to show you our **capital** city. Just think, here I am in the presence of the five regional winners of the President's National Geography Bee. *(points to Denzel)* Would you mind introducing the group?

DENZEL: *(points to each person as named)* Sure, I'll introduce everyone. My name is Denzel, and I live in San Francisco, California. This is Peter from New York City. Lila is from Atlanta, Georgia. Jen is from St. Louis, Missouri. And Roberto is from Tucson, Arizona.

TOUR GUIDE: Great! Now let me tell you what we'll be doing for the next three days. We'll begin our first day of touring with a visit to the Mall.

JEN: *(jokingly)* The mall? Are we going shopping?

ROBERTO: Very funny. We are not going to a shopping mall. We're going to see the Mall.

www.harcourtschoolsupply.com
© Harcourt Achieve Inc. All rights reserved.

105

It's a Capital Idea!
Readers' Theater 5, SV 9781419031700

PETER: It's sort of like an open-air museum. It's where all the **monuments** to the presidents are located.

TOUR GUIDE: That's exactly right. We will see many important sites. And we may see some important people in this great city.

LILA: You mean we might run into the president?

TOUR GUIDE: That's right, Lila. You never know whom you might see. Now, let's get the tour started! Our tour van is right over there. *(Pointing to a van.)*

LILA: *(stepping out of the van)* Hey, isn't that the Washington Monument over there? It sure is tall!

JEN: It looks like a really tall, skinny pyramid.

PETER: That is indeed the Washington Monument. It's over 550 feet tall. And it is modeled after an ancient Egyptian design, so maybe that's why you think it looks like a pyramid.

ROBERTO: Is there anything you don't know, Peter?

www.harcourtschoolsupply.com
© Harcourt Achieve Inc. All rights reserved.

106

It's a Capital Idea!
Readers' Theater 5, SV 9781419031700

Tour Guide: Why don't we take the elevator to the top? From there we'll be able to see the Lincoln **Memorial**, the Jefferson Memorial, the White House, and the **Capitol** building.

Denzel: *(steps forward into the elevator)* Hey, Peter, maybe you can answer this question: Why does the Washington Monument look like it's two different colors?

Peter *(steps forward into the elevator)* Oh, that's an easy one. The Washington Monument was planned back in the late 1700s by L'Enfant (lawn FAWN), the original **architect**. But construction did not begin until 1848 and wasn't completed for thirty years after that. So, the marble came from different places at different times— that's why the colors are different.

Lila: *(waving the group over)* Come look at this view. It's truly breathtaking!

Roberto: It sure is. I think you can see all of Washington!

Tour Guide: Everyone look across the Reflecting Pool toward the Lincoln Memorial. That will be our next stop.

> **FLUENCY TIP**
>
> Remember to pause at commas and dashes and chunk sentences into phrases.

It's a Capital Idea!
Readers' Theater 5, SV 9781419031700

PETER: The Reflecting Pool contains over seven million gallons of water.

DENZEL: You're like a walking encyclopedia, aren't you?

LILA: *(bumping into a man)* Excuse me, sir.

JEN: *(pointing back toward the elevator)* Hey, did you see that group of guys that got on the elevator after us? They were all wearing sunglasses and dressed in black. I wonder who they were.

DENZEL: They looked sort of suspicious. Maybe they were spies!

LILA: I don't know who they were, but the one who bumped into me looked a bit familiar. I just can't place him, though.

ROBERTO: Maybe they were Secret Service agents.

JEN: Like the ones who guard the president? Why would the president be here?

TOUR GUIDE: *(waving them to the base of the Lincoln Memorial)* This is the most-visited monument on the Mall. I'd like everyone to read one of the passages inscribed on the memorial's wall. Remember these are the very steps where Dr. Martin Luther King, Jr., gave his famous "I Have a Dream" speech in 1963.

It's a Capital Idea!
Readers' Theater 5, SV 9781419031700

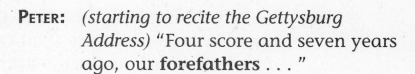

PETER: *(starting to recite the Gettysburg Address)* "Four score and seven years ago, our **forefathers** . . . "

(Everyone pauses to read the Gettysburg Address.)

LILA: Are we going to visit the Vietnam Veterans Memorial? I thought that was on the Mall, too.

ROBERTO: Yeah. I'd like to see that. My uncle was killed in the Vietnam War. I would like to find his name on the wall.

TOUR GUIDE: We'll come back after lunch to see the Vietnam Veterans Memorial. There are more than 58,000 names on the wall. It will take us some time to find Roberto's uncle.

(The next morning arrives.)

✳ TOUR GUIDE: Good morning! We'll start the day with a private tour of the White House, and then we'll sit in on a special session of Congress at the Capitol building. Next stop: 1600 Pennsylvania Avenue!

JEN: *(while standing in the Lincoln Bedroom on their White House tour)* Was this actually Lincoln's bedroom while he was president?

> **✳ FLUENCY TIP**
>
> A colon reminds us to pause. Notice the colon in the Tour Guide's part.

www.harcourtschoolsupply.com
109
It's a Capital Idea!
Readers' Theater 5, SV 9781419031700

PETER: No, it was his office. The office the president uses now—the Oval Office— didn't exist back in Lincoln's time.

TOUR GUIDE: Right again, Peter. Now let's head over to the Oval Office. We have a few minutes before we have to leave for the Capitol.

ROBERTO: *(pointing to a man walking down the hall away from the group)* Isn't that the same guy we keep seeing all over Washington?

DENZEL: It looks like the same man. Who is he, and why is he following us?

TOUR GUIDE: *(walking out of the Capitol with the group)* I certainly liked the president's speech. I hope each of you did, too.

JEN: Yes, and it sure solved a mystery, didn't it?

LILA: I can't believe that the president does that before every important speech. He visits the monuments and memorials to help him remember all the great things about our country.

DENZEL: *(laughing)* And we thought the President of the United States was a spy!

> **FLUENCY TIP**
>
> Remember that if a sentence doesn't make sense, try reading it differently.

It's a Capital Idea!
Readers' Theater 5, SV 9781419031700

Comprehension

Write your answer to each question on the lines below.

1. What do the five students on the tour have in common?

_____

_____

2. Why does Denzel think the group of men are spies?

_____

_____

3. Why do you think the Lincoln Memorial is the most-visited monument on the Mall? _____

_____

4. What do the students do while visiting the Capitol?

_____

_____

5. What monument looks like "a tall, skinny pyramid"?

_____

_____

6. Why does the Washington Monument have different colors of marble?

_____

_____

7. What building or memorial would you most like to visit in Washington, D.C.? Why? _____

_____

www.harcourtschoolsupply.com
© Harcourt Achieve Inc. All rights reserved.

111

It's a Capital Idea!
Readers' Theater 5, SV 9781419031700

Vocabulary

Write the vocabulary word that answers the question.

> memorial   Capitol   capital   forefathers   architect   monument

1. Which word describes an important city in every state? _____

2. What building is home to U.S. lawmakers? _____

3. Which word describes your great-great-grandparents? _____

4. What do you call a person who designs buildings? _____

5. Which two words describe something built to honor a person or event?

_____   _____

Extension

1. With a partner, talk about the questions you asked yourself during the play "It's a Capital Idea!"

- Were you surprised by the play's ending?

- What clues in the play helped you figure out what the ending might be?

- Were there any words you were unsure about?

2. Research a Washington, D.C., building, monument, or memorial.

- Design a poster that will make visitors to Washington, D.C., want to see the building, monument, or memorial you are describing.

- Share your research and poster with your classmates.

www.harcourtschoolsupply.com
© Harcourt Achieve Inc. All rights reserved.

112

It's a Capital Idea!
Readers' Theater 5, SV 9781419031700

Racing the Iditarod

Summary

"Racing the Iditarod" is a six-character play about three mushers in the Iditarod and the reporters who are covering the race.

Meet the Players

Character	Reading Level
Narrator	5.4
Reporter Bob	6.1
Reporter Chi	4.8
Racer Dan	3.7
Racer Nadia	2.9
Racer Baral	3.4

Fluency Focus
Using Expression

Comprehension Focus
Visualizing

Vocabulary
bitter
ceremonial
mandatory
musher
official
stupendous
tundra
whiteout

Read Aloud Tip

Introduce the fluency focus of **using expression**. Explain that fluent readers stress important words by reading them in a stronger voice. Direct students to listen as you reread paragraph 2, noting which words you stress. Then read, stressing such words as *symbols*, *family*, *history*, *story*, *honor*, and *pride*.

Set the Stage

Teacher Read Aloud *page 115*

This selection is about totem poles. Read the selection aloud. As you do, model good fluency, reading smoothly, and stressing important words. For example, in paragraph 1, you might stress the words *artists*, *special*, *carvings*, *misunderstood*, *frighten*, *never*, and *totem poles*.

Get Ready

Vocabulary *page 116*

Use this page to introduce vocabulary. Discuss the Vocabulary Think Tank question, asking students to explain what makes their example mandatory.

Fluency and Comprehension Warm-Ups *pages 116–117*

Review these pages with students. Use the following for students who need additional help with the concepts:

- **Using Expression** To make your reading more expressive, stress important words by stretching them out or saying them more loudly. What words would you stress in the first sentence of paragraph 3 of the Read Aloud?

- **Visualizing** Visualizing is creating mental pictures as you read. Think about what your senses would tell you if you were part of a scene. For example, when the Read Aloud describes placing a totem pole, you might feel the weight of the pole and hear the music and voices at the ceremony.

Racing the Iditarod *pages 118–124*

Independent Practice

Set up the groups and assign each student a part. Then have students read through their assigned parts once before small group practice begins.

Small Group Practice

Assemble the groups. You may want to use the following rehearsal schedule. Each rehearsal, which should involve a complete oral read-through, has an activity to guide students.

1. First Rehearsal: Invite students to scan the entire play to find italicized stage directions. Point out that these directions tell actors how to speak or what to do. Then ask students to read together as a group for the first time.

2. Vocabulary Rehearsal: Ask students to locate and list the play's vocabulary words. Have each student choose one word and write a riddle that can be answered by the word. For example, a riddle for the word *tundra* might be: *You can walk on me. I am flat and cold. What am I?* Allow students to trade riddles.

3. Fluency Rehearsal: Using Expression Review the Fluency Warm-Up on page 116 and the Fluency Tips on pages 120, 122, and 124. Remind students to consider the characters' feelings and to use their voices to express them. After the reading, ask students to work in their groups to locate and read in unison sentences that express excitement, fear, pain, and happiness.

4. Comprehension Rehearsal: Visualizing Guide students to focus on creating pictures in their minds as they read. After the reading, ask them each to draw one scene or event they visualized. Have students share their drawings.

5. Final Rehearsal: Observe this rehearsal, focusing on students' expression. For example, does Nadia sound upset or in pain when she says, "Ouch! I chipped a tooth on that bump!"?

Performance

This is your opportunity to sit back, relax, and enjoy the performance. Encourage students to have fun while performing!

Curtain Call *pages 125–126*

Assign these questions and activities for students to complete independently or in a group.

Vocabulary Tip

For more vocabulary practice, have students discuss the following:

- How would you dress for **bitter** weather?

- Would the **tundra** be a good place for a farm? Why or why not?

- Name an **official** you might see at a baseball game.

Set the Stage

Teacher Read Aloud

Long ago, artists in Native American clans along the southeastern coast of Alaska began making special carvings for their people. Early European explorers often misunderstood what the carved poles meant. They guessed that the figures on the poles were meant to frighten visitors or to be worshiped. This was never true. Today, we call these carvings totem poles.

Totem poles in Alaska have always been symbols. Many of the traditional carvings are about an owner's family or clan history. Others tell a story or honor a person. Their meaning is a source of great pride.

Today, some totem poles are still being created as they were in the past. Traditionally, each pole is usually made from a cedar tree and carved over many months. The owner decides what figures should be shown; the lead carver decides the figures' details and whether to paint them. As many as 100 clan members carry the finished pole to a deep hole and help set it in place. Then a very important ceremony is held. The owner tells the meaning of the figures and everyone joins in feasting, music, dancing, and gift giving.

In this play, you will learn more about Alaska. Use the vocabulary and warm-ups to help you get ready.

Vocabulary

Read and review these words to prepare you for reading this play. Say each word aloud to a friend two times.

bitter—very cold

ceremonial—something for a special occasion

mandatory—required

musher—the person who drives a dog sled

official—formal, with authority

stupendous—amazing

tundra—a flat, treeless plain with frozen ground

whiteout—a snowstorm that blocks all sight

> **VOCABULARY THINK TANK**
>
> What is an example of something that is mandatory?

Fluency Warm-Up:

Using Expression

Fluent readers use **expression**. You need to think about how characters would feel as they speak. Changing your voice on important words helps show feeling. You can "be" the character with your voice and face!

Remember to use a higher voice to end questions and show excitement or happiness. Use a lower voice to show fear or sadness. Say important words longer, louder, or with a different voice.

FLUENCY PRACTICE

Read each sentence three times. Use your voice to first sound sad, then happy, and then really excited.

1. A wolf is howling just over the next hill.

2. Our experiment had different results than we expected.

3. Mom says we will go to a big city on our vacation.

Comprehension Warm-Up

Visualizing

Imagine yourself in the middle of a story's action! You can make a picture in your mind as if you see everything and everyone around you. This is called **visualizing**, and it helps you really understand the characters and events.

Remember to pause to think about what you are reading. Use your mind to imagine what the characters are thinking and feeling.

COMPREHENSION TIP

As you read, ask yourself questions like these to help you visualize the story's characters and events.

1. What would I see, hear, feel, and smell in this setting?

2. Is this action like events I've seen or read about before?

3. How would I feel if I were this character?

Readers' Theater

Presents

Racing the Iditarod

by

Jerrill Parham

Cast

(in order of appearance)

Narrator _____

Reporter Bob _____

Reporter Chi _____

Racer Dan _____

Racer Nadia _____

Racer Baral _____

NARRATOR: The famous Iditarod Sled Dog Race has begun! Last Saturday, 70 teams, each with one hopeful **musher** and 12 to 16 strong dogs, left the starting line in Anchorage. The start of the race was **ceremonial**.

BOB: We are here at Wasilla on Sunday. Yesterday, the teams raced to Eagle River and then came here by truck for the **official** time start. Everyone feels **stupendous** excitement! Look at the dogs leaping. They are ready to run!

CHI: Bob and I will fly to checkpoints and speak with three mushers during the race. Let's quickly meet them now. Here are Dan, Nadia, and Baral.

DAN: Hello. This is my second Iditarod. Some of my dogs ran it with my father another time. I'm racing to see how the dogs and I have improved as a team. We've spent almost every day this year getting ready.

Readers' Theater 5, SV 9781419031700

NADIA: This is my team's first Iditarod, but my dogs have won shorter races. Sled dog races are really about the dogs, you know. I'm like every other musher here, because I really know my dogs.

BARAL: My dogs and I like being together in nature. This is our third Iditarod. We are ready to face anything. Nature makes surprises in Alaska!

BOB: The racers will be on the Iditarod Trail for days. This year, mushers must check in and out at 23 places before reaching Nome. Nome is about 1,060 miles away! Many teams won't finish.

NARRATOR: Now, back to our mushers.

NADIA: *(bumping up and down)* Bumps and more bumps are in these swamps and forests. First I yell "Gee" to go right and then "Haw" to go left. Toby and Streak are being good lead dogs. Ouch! I chipped a tooth on that bump!

FLUENCY TIP

Make your voice and face show excitement in the right places.

Readers' Theater 5, SV 9781419031700

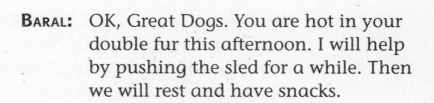

BARAL: OK, Great Dogs. You are hot in your double fur this afternoon. I will help by pushing the sled for a while. Then we will rest and have snacks.

DAN: The ties seem to be holding the sled's bar together. We did not need the bad spill we took on a turn back there. But you're OK. That is what matters.

CHI: Here we are at mile 145 of the trail. Our teams made good time across some flat, frozen lakes and rivers.

BARAL: *(twists his body as he talks)* We will twist and turn uphill through trees. But coming down is the hard part. I will ride on the brake so the sled doesn't hit my dogs.

NARRATOR: Nadia is on her way through the pass area.

NADIA: *(tipping right, then left)* Here's the scariest cliff yet! . . . We must CREEP to stay safe! . . . Uh-oh! It's time to tip the sled onto only the right runner . . . and now the left!

BOB: I'm happy to report that our three teams made it here to mile 303. A few other teams are dropping out of the race. What happened, mushers?

BARAL: We just had a beautiful night run with the bright moon. Of course, that was AFTER we got through the blowing snow of the **tundra**.

DAN: I could only see the tall trail markers—not the dogs! I led the dogs sometimes.

CHI: We are at mile 571 now, where a **mandatory** 8-hour rest begins. As our teams arrive, I'll ask about their latest challenges.

NADIA: We slid across slick, frozen waters. Then we went through the LONGEST, EMPTIEST, LONELIEST areas I've ever seen! The only sounds were wolf howls. AOOOOOOO!

DAN: I melted snow for us to drink. A **whiteout** was bad but quick. When we were wet, we just had to keep moving to dry so we wouldn't freeze. BRRR! *(Shivers.)*

BOB: This is mile 986. Whew! Teams had a hard time on the Yukon River. Then they pushed on along the **bitter** Bering Sea coast. Nadia, how was it?

> ❋ **FLUENCY TIP**
>
> Change your voice or speed to emphasize one or more important words in each sentence. Be sure to emphasize words with all capitalized letters.

NADIA: I could not get used to hearing the sea ice crack under us. The wind chill was so bad that I put some dog booties inside my face mask.

CHI: We hear that only 40 teams are still in this race. Baral began racing again before dawn.

BARAL: *(racing again)* OK, Great Dogs. It's day 10, the day we get to Nome! We are making it through the last wind and bitter cold. Soon we will see wild musk oxen. We are getting close to Nome.

NARRATOR: Later, Dan and Nadia are in the last stretch.

DAN: *(racing)* Baral and others left long before us. They've probably passed under the ceremonial arch at the finish.

CHI: We're standing near the arch in Nome. Baral, your team's official finish was in sixth place. Are you happy about that?

BARAL: Yes! Finishing in any place is terrific. Finishing in the top ten or twenty places is really special.

Readers' Theater 5, SV 9781419031700

BOB: We have late-breaking news from the radio spotter car. Dan and Nadia's teams are running neck and neck down the final stretch! The dogs seem to be flying, and the mushers are grinning.

NARRATOR: Nadia's lead dogs pass under the arch just five SECONDS before Dan's! The teams finish in ninth and tenth places.

BOB: Wow! Let's get the scoop. Mushers, after ten days of almost unbelievable challenges, will you ever enter the Iditarod again?

BARAL: I've made plans all along the way for next year's race.

DAN: Me, too. My dogs and I will be back, stronger than ever.

NADIA: Of course! Just watch us next year!

FLUENCY TIP

Practice reading sentences of fear, happiness, and excitement on pages 123 and 124.

Comprehension

Write your answer to each question on the lines below.

1. What are the starting and ending points of the Iditarod?

_____

_____

2. Why is it harder going downhill than uphill?

_____

_____

3. Why do you think the teams must take mandatory eight-hour rests?

_____

_____

4. Why did Dan, Nadia, and Baral enter the race?

_____

_____

5. What do people do to keep the dogs as safe as possible?

_____

_____

6. Explain at least two things that you learned about Alaska from reading

this play. _____

_____

7. Would you rather participate in or watch the Iditarod? Why?

_____

_____

Readers' Theater 5, SV 9781419031700

Vocabulary

Finish the paragraph by writing a vocabulary word on each line.

stupendous	tundra	ceremonial	official
whiteout	bitter	mandatory	musher

The dogs surged forward, eager to be on their way. Brisk winds

had caused a (1) _____, which had forced

Nadine to stop until she could see the trail. But now the sled flew

over the icy (2) _____. Nadine forgot about the

(3) _____ cold. This whole experience had been

absolutely (4) _____. And now it looked as if she

would be the first (5) _____ to reach the finish line.

Extension

1. Imagine yourself as a musher in the Iditarod Sled Dog Race. With a partner, talk about these questions.

   • What would you think about before, during, and after the race?

   • What might be your biggest challenge? Why?

   • What could you enjoy in the race?

2. Work with a partner to research one of the topics below that interests you. Then present your findings to the class.

   • An Alaskan Native American tribe

   • Animals and plants of the Alaskan tundra

   • Denali or Gates of the Arctic National Park

   • A city in Alaska

Answer Key

The Rescue

Comprehension, page 27

(Suggested responses)

1. The family is visiting Sri Lanka because Mom has to be there on business.
2. They hear an awful noise and see people running.
3. A tsunami is a giant wave that's often caused by an earthquake far out at sea.
4. Responses will vary.
5. I visualize rushing water covering all the ground around the hotel.
6. They tie sheets together, lower them down to Mom, and then pull her up into the hotel.
7. Responses will vary.

Vocabulary, page 28

1. surge
2. frantic
3. debris
4. destruction
5. eternity

Science Alive

Comprehension, page 41

(Suggested responses)

1. Skin is the largest organ of the human body. It covers us and protects us from germs.
2. Melanin gives our skin its color and protects us from the sun.
3. People get goose bumps because blood vessels narrow to keep the body warm.
4. You can keep your skin healthy by using sunscreen and by keeping it clean.
5. Responses will vary.
6. Responses will vary.

Vocabulary, page 42

1. germs
2. organ
3. infection
4. virus, bacteria
5. Melanin

The W.H.A.T.E.V.E.R.

Comprehension, page 55

(Suggested responses)

1. The machine must be a compound machine, and it must use at least two forms of kinetic energy.
2. The machine uses chemical energy when it fills the balloon with carbon dioxide.
3. Larger blades mean Nick doesn't have to blow as hard.
4. The marble is so heavy that it breaks the egg instead of cracking it.
5. Responses will vary.
6. Responses will vary.
7. The simple machines are the ramp (lever) and the teeter-totter (lever). The kinetic energy is in the falling object.

Vocabulary, page 56

Answers from top to bottom should read as follows:
5, 3, 1, 7, 6, 2, 4

A Boston Teapot

Comprehension, page 69

(Suggested responses)

1. The colonists refuse to pay the tax on tea because they do not have anyone to represent them in Parliament.
2. Participants disguise themselves because they are afraid that they will be hanged if they are caught.
3. The phrase "taxation without representation" means that the colonists are taxed by England without having a say in the English government.
4. The colonists first try to return the tea because they hope to solve the problem peacefully.
5. Responses will vary.

6. One thing that happened because of the tea party was that Boston Harbor was closed.
7. Responses will vary.

Vocabulary, page 70

Answers from top to bottom should read as follows:
4, 3, 6, 2, 1, 7, 5

The Railroad Race

Comprehension, page 83

(Suggested responses)

1. Two dangers workers faced were working on steep slopes and getting away from lit fuses.
2. Native Americans were angry that the railroad was cutting through their land and that workers were killing a lot of buffalo.
3. The roadbed must be higher than the ground so rain won't wash it out.
4. The final spike was made of gold as a symbol that it was important.
5. Responses will vary.
6. The transcontinental railroad was built to bind the country together and to connect the railroads in the East to California.
7. Responses will vary.

Vocabulary, page 84

1. transcontinental
2. telegraph
3. surveyor
4. tough
5. spectacular

Answer Key
Readers' Theater 5, SV 9781419031700

The Hills Are Alive

Comprehension, page 97

(Suggested responses)
1. Kim wants to show the man that she doesn't have much money.
2. Kim and Lin think the men are wearing costumes and that they aren't really the presidents.
3. The story about Washington and the cherry tree wasn't true.
4. Responses will vary.
5. The presidents learn that leeches are no longer being used by doctors to treat disease. Pills and other medicines are used instead.
6. Responses will vary.
7. Responses will vary.

Vocabulary, page 98

1. leeches
2. Memorial
3. portrait
4. extraordinary
5. nickname

It's a Capital Idea!

Comprehension, page 111

(Suggested responses)
1. All the students won prizes in the National Geography Bee.
2. The men are all dressed in black and wear sunglasses.
3. Responses will vary.
4. The students listen to the president give a speech.
5. The Washington Monument looks like a tall, skinny pyramid.
6. The Washington Monument has different colors of marble because the marble came from different places at different times.
7. Responses will vary.

Vocabulary, page 112

1. capital
2. Capitol
3. forefathers
4. architect
5. memorial, monument

Racing the Iditarod

Comprehension, page 125

(Suggested responses)
1. The Iditarod starts in Anchorage and ends in Nome.
2. When the teams go downhill, the sled can hit the dogs.
3. The dogs and mushers need rest to be able to race safely.
4. Dan entered the race to see how his dogs and he have improved as a team. Nadia entered the race because her dogs had won shorter races and she probably wants to see how well they do in a longer race. Baral entered the race because he and his dogs like being together in nature.
5. To keep the dogs as safe as possible, people help them keep cool when they are too hot, use the brake going downhill so the sled doesn't hit the dogs, go slow in dangerous places, allow them to rest, melt snow for them to drink, and put booties on their feet.
6. Responses will vary.
7. Responses will vary.

Vocabulary, page 126

1. whiteout
2. tundra
3. bitter
4. stupendous
5. musher

Answer Key
Readers' Theater 5, SV 9781419031700